THE RIBBLE WAY

The Ribble Way

THE RIBBLE WAY

A 70-mile recreational footpath close to the
banks of the river from sea to source.

BY

GLADYS SELLERS

ROUTE MAPS DRAWN BY JOHN WILSON PARKER
ILLUSTRATIONS BY R.BRIAN EVANS

CICERONE PRESS
2 POLICE SQUARE, MILNTHORPE, CUMBRIA

© Gladys Sellers 1985
ISBN 1 85284 107 9
First published 1985
Reprint 1986
Second Edition 1993

British Library Cataloguing-in-Publication Data. A catalogue record is
available for this book from the British Library.

Advice to Readers

Readers are advised that whilst every effort is taken by the author
to ensure the accuracy of this guidebook, changes can occur
which may affect the contents. It is advisable to check locally on
transport, accommodation, shops etc but even rights-of-way can
be altered and, more especially overseas, paths can be eradicated
by landslip, forest fires or changes of ownership.

The publisher would welcome notes of any such changes

Front Cover: The Ribble at Dinckley
Photo: Brian Evans

CONTENTS

Acknowledgements 6

The Way in Brief 7

The Story of the Ribble Way 9

The Source of the Ribble 12

The Fair Face of Ribblesdale 14

Before You Start 21

The Way in Detail:

Section 1:	Longton to Penwortham Bridge, Preston 27
Section 2:	Penwortham Bridge to Brockholes Bridge, Preston 34
Section 3:	Brockholes Bridge to Ribchester 40
Section 4:	Ribchester to Brungerley Bridge, Clitheroe 49
Section 4a:	Optional Diversion to Stonyhurst College 62
Section 5:	Brungerley Bridge, Clitheroe, to Gisburn 65
Section 6:	Gisburn to Settle 75
Section 7:	Settle to Horton-in-Ribblesdale 86
Section 8:	Horton-in-Ribblesdale to the source 92

ACKNOWLEDGEMENTS

I should like to express my sincere thanks to the following people: Mr D.Sutherland and Mrs Alison Heine for many helpful conversations on progress and for providing me with detailed maps of the route in Lancashire; Mr R.Lonsdale and Ms Sue Arnott of the Yorkshire Dales National Park for much useful information about path diversion orders and facilities within the Park; Mr T.Clarkson and Mr A.Howard of the Preston and Fylde Group of the Ramblers' Association for the history of the Ribble Way; Mr N.Turner, Curator of the Castle Museum, Clitheroe, for a private tour of that museum and for clarifying the geology of the Ribble Valley for me; and last but not least, Mrs Elsie Baines of Walton-le-Dale for allowing me access to her extensive notes about Ribblesdale.

Gladys Sellers

Pen-y-ghent from the Ribble Way at Helwith Bridge. Here the Settle-Carlisle railway crosses the river

THE WAY IN BRIEF

Since the first edition of this book was written several major changes and many minor ones have been made. Others are in the pipeline and the most important one is the revival, in the summer of 1991, of the plans to build a footbridge over the Hodder close to its confluence with the Ribble. In the early days of planning the Ribble Way, this bridge was the preferred alternative to the Calder bridge, which in the event was not built either. When built it will not only eliminate the dangerous length of road to Great Mitton, but open up a superb length of river to walkers. At some future date there may have to be a major change of route at Sawley, for the landowner there is contesting the right of way through the gorge to Gisburn. The route of the Way can never, it seems, be regarded as final, but here is a summary of it as it was in the summer of 1991.

The Way starts near Longton, close the river's mouth, and, having joined the marsh banks, follows them and then the river embankment to Penwortham Bridge. It then skirts the town of Preston through Broadgate, Miller and Avenham Parks, and follows the banks of the river to Brockholes Bridge. Here the Way leaves the river banks and cuts across country well above river level to the outskirts of Ribchester, from which it uses the road (B6245) to Ribchester Bridge. From here it follows the river for about a mile and then climbs up to cut off a large bend and comes back to it at Dinckley Footbridge. After a brief diversion inland the Way again follows the river to its confluence with the Hodder, where it makes a big diversion to cross that river at Lower Hodder Bridge, reaching Great Mitton by a length of unpleasant and dangerous road. The route continues, more or less on the river bank, to Grindleton Bridge, Clitheroe. Soon after this bridge it leaves the river bank and does a short stretch on the road to regain the Ribble's bank just beyond Sawley, then follows the river through a superb wooded gorge almost to Gisburn. Beyond Gisburn the Way follows the Hellifield road (A682) almost to Paythorne, then goes cross country, not regaining the banks of the Ribble except very briefly until the outskirts of Settle.

From Langcliffe the Way follows the bank to Stainforth, then climbs high over the moor to reach Helwith Bridge as there are no right of way paths along the Ribble. From here it follows the banks of the Ribble to the bridge at Horton-in-Ribblesdale. At Horton the route follows the pastures well above river level to Nether Lodge, then cuts direct over rough ground to the Ingleton-Hawes road. In order to avoid a busy road the Way now utilises the Dales Way as far as Newby Head, then follows Jam Sike to the source.

A return to Horton-in-Ribblesdale by the Pennine Way is suggested, or, if the time of day be right, divert to Ribblehead Station by taking the right fork on Cam End to the Ribblehead-Hawes road which you reach a good mile from the station. See Yorkshire Dales Outdoor Leisure Map No.2.

THE STORY OF THE RIBBLE WAY

The Ribble Way is without a doubt the brain child of the Preston and Fylde group of the Ramblers' Association, for at its inaugural meeting in 1967, the all important suggestion was made.

"We've got a Pennine Way," they said, "Why not work for a Ribble Way?" The idea was taken up with enthusiasm. There was no doubt that it was a worthwhile one because of the large numbers of people living close to the Ribble Valley.

The valley was surveyed by members of the newly formed group in order to work out a route giving the best walking and, joined by members of the North East Lancashire Area of the Ramblers' Association in whose territory much of the route lay, they devised one that followed the banks of the Ribble from the sea to Far Gearstones, a total 64 miles. In many places right of way paths did not exist along the banks of the river so fishermen's paths were used, for they felt that to depart widely from the banks would lose the unique atmosphere of a riverside walk that was an essential part of the Ribble Way. The proposed route needed some 36 miles of new right of way paths. This early work took a great deal of time, and it was not until 1972 that the Ramblers were able to approach their national body with a proposal for the creation of a long distance footpath to be called The Ribble Way. The national body of the R.A. in turn approached the Countryside Commission and made a release to the Press. Not surprisingly the press release brought unfavourable comment and opposition from the Bowlands Rural District Council and from the National Farmers Union.

For several years very little happened until in 1980 the newly formed Mid Lancashire Area of the Ramblers' Association joined with the North East Lancashire Area to form a Ribble Way Committee. This committee set to work to devise a route which would be acceptable to the people who had objected so strongly to the original proposal. It was decided to shorten the route to end at Paythorne, close to the Lancashire County boundary. This meant that the whole of the route was now in Lancashire and in the territories of the two Ramblers' Association Areas concerned. This shortened route required only $19^{1}/_{2}$ miles of new right of way compared with the original proposal's 36. In March 1980 the Ribble Way Committee issued a proposal for The Ribble Way as a recreational footpath, describing the route in some detail, and in April 1980 the Countryside Commission convened a meeting to discuss their proposals. They invited the Lancashire branch of the N.F.U., the Country Landowners Association, Preston Borough Council, South Ribble Borough Council, Ribble Valley Borough Council, Lancashire County Council, and, obviously, the Mid Lancashire Area and North East Lancashire Area of the R.A. Again, there was considerable opposition by some of the bodies present though others were in favour, but it became clear that the establishment of the Ribble Way would depend on its using existing right of way paths almost entirely. For those who had worked so hard to open up the many fishermen's paths that gave such high quality walking this spelt defeat. More surveys were done and a composite route designed and called 'The Interim Ribble Way,' signifying that all hope had not been abandoned even at this stage. The new route certainly offered compensations: there were excellent views up the valley that the riverside paths lacked.

In July 1982, as part of a nationwide campaign called 'Discover your local footpaths' organised by the national body of the R.A., the Interim Ribble Way was launched. R.A. members led a series of guided walks during the weekend of July 31st/August 1st to gain publicity for the scheme and sent letters to the Countryside Commission and the Lancashire County Council. Now the wheel of fortune changed: officialdom expressed interest and eventually the Countryside Commission agreed to provide financial help while the Lancashire County Council undertook to carry out the work to improve stiles and footbridges where needed and to mark the route with the logo designed by a member of the Ribble Way Committee and displayed on the title page of this book. Before work started the Lancashire County Council held discussions with the Ramblers' Association to make some minor modifications to the route. It was agreed that it should end at Gisburn, much better placed for public services than Paythorne, and to start at Longton to avoid expensive bridge works on the marsh banks required by the Much Hoole starting point. The original route walked the north bank of the Ribble between Ribchester and Great Mitton and required a new bridge over the Hodder at its junction with the Ribble and a subsequent mile or more of new right of way path. The alternatives were for people to walk the road, busy and dangerous, or to transfer the route to the south bank at Dinckley footbridge. This route required a bridge over the Calder but as it would be a less expensive structure than the proposed Hodder Bridge and as no new right of way paths were needed, this route was chosen. An opening ceremony by Mike Harding, President of the Ramblers' Association, and Sir Derek Barber, Chairman of the Countryside Commission, took place on June 1st 1985 at Edisford Bridge, Clitheroe.

The Mid and North East Lancashire Areas of the Ramblers' Association obviously hoped that this truncated Ribble Way would one day be extended to the original finishing point, but they accepted that this work would have to be undertaken by people living closer to the scene than their members.

In fact this extension was achieved much more speedily than expected. Cicerone Press gave the author a free hand to devise a route beyond Gisburn in the hope that it would gain official recognition at some future date. She chose to go to the source, the logical conclusion; reasons for her choice are given in the next chapter. This development came to the notice of the Yorkshire Dales National Park and the North Yorkshire County Council through whose territories the extension passes, and they both expressed considerable interest. The Countryside Commission provided additional grant aid for this purpose. The Yorkshire Dales National Park undertook to keep an eye on paths subject to additional wear and to signpost the Way wherever it crossed a road.

The entire Ribble Way thus gained official recognition early in 1985.

THE SOURCE OF THE RIBBLE

A river rarely has just one indisputable source and the selection of one of the many springs that form the headwaters of the Ribble poses questions of geography and history. The Ordnance Survey uses the word 'Ribblehead' implying source to the area where the river becomes known as Thorns Gill. This is too vague to be satisfactory and is at variance with the dictionary definition of the word source. Geographers make their selection by assessing the length and volume of water contributed by various tributaries and the altitude at which they rise.

In the past other writers have made their choice. Let us consider them. At Whitsuntide 1862 William Dobson, who wrote the book *Rambles by the Ribble,* made a little expedition - for that is what it was in those days - to find the source of the Ribble. He claimed it was on Wold Fell. 'There are two springs on Wold Fell and their commingling waters form a tolerable brook when they reach the roadside. The highest of them is only about three to four hundred yards from the highway. We regard it as *the* source of the Ribble.' The highway, he makes clear, is the highest point of the Ingleton-Hawes road. Frederick Riley, writing in 1914 in *The Ribble from Source to Sea,* mentions the geographical desiderata and allows the reader to take his pick. If the name is important, then the source is at Gearstones, if altitude is important, then the source is on Cam Fell, if furthest from the sea, a spring on Wold Fell. Jessica Lofthouse, who was quite a walker in her younger days, discusses the alternatives in her book *The Three Rivers* (1949). She considers a spring high on Cam Fell to be one of the 'headsprings' because of its altitude. On the other hand she describes a spring high on Wold Fell as 'the source'. This surely is the same one described by both Dobson and Riley. In more recent times Wainwright in his *Ribble Sketchbook* pays no heed to geographical niceties. He settles for the roadside junction of Long Gill and Ouster Gill.

The present author feels the need to satisfy geographic constraints more strongly than the need to conform with historical tradition. However, the overriding requirement is to select a spring which can be reached by following a right of way path along the banks of its stream. There is only one candidate: the springs at the head of Jam Syke on Gayle Wold. These springs satisfy the geographical requirement admirably. They are marginally higher than either the Cam End or Wold Fell springs and do not dry up in drought. The highest of them burbles forth in a most satisfying manner from the base of a little limestone cliff. As far as this book is concerned, this spring is *the* source.

THE FAIR FACE OF RIBBLESDALE

For a great many years now Ribblesdale has been dear to the hearts of all Lancastrians who love good countryside. Many are the writers who have described its charms and beauties. This is not a pale imitation of them, but looks at the reasons for the valley's attractiveness.

Rock structures and types are the basis of all scenery, of fundamental importance in assessing the changes that occur in the landscape. Obviously there are big changes in rock types along the length of the valley. All around Preston to just east of the M6 the rock is a warm, red sandstone, Buntner Sandstone, for the technically minded. It is exposed by river erosion close to Brockholes and the walker can see how Red Scar Wood gets its name. Beyond this point the rocks are those of the Millstone Grit Series, very much older and harder than the Buntner Sandstones around Preston. Hard rocks tend to give bold features in the landscape, and they now appear - Longridge Fell on the north side of the valley, the West Pennine Moors on the south, and continue to Whalley Nab and Pendle Hill. The rocks of the valley floor change again near Dinckley to the Worston Shales. These shales are lime-bearing and produce better soils than the gritstones, even though their effect is masked to a considerable extent by a thick layer of boulder clay left by the retreating glaciers of the last Ice Age.

Throughout the length of the river's flood plain, well seen in many places all the way to Sawley, the soils are alluvial, deposits of river silt made by floods over the last few thousand years. These rich soils produce the lush grasses needed by today's high yield dairy farming.

Around Clitheroe bands of limestone appear in the landscape, used to build the unmistakable grey-white houses. This is Chatburn Limestone, brought to the surface by the faulting which accompanied the raising of the anticlyne on which Clitheroe and this part of the valley stands. It is a much darker limestone than the Great Scar Limestone found beyond Settle.

Clitheroe Castle however is built on a reef knoll, another type of limestone, not so dark and rather friable. There are a whole series of reef knolls running in a north-easterly direction through Worston, beyond Skipton into the western edge of Wharfedale. They are thought to be the remains of a coral reef. Chatburn Limestone is responsible for the most dramatic feature of the Ribble Way, the gorge between Sawley and Gisburn. Here a wedge of hard Chatburn Limestone obtrudes into the Worston Shales, and, being so much harder than the shales, has resisted the tendency of the river to wander about and has directed its energies downwards.

Beyond the gorge the Worston Shales ensure that the valley resumes its former characteristics, then near Wigglesworth they give way to Millstone Grits. This is no longer fence and hedgerow country, but stone wall country, for gritstones make good building stone. The South Craven Fault caused the disappearance of these rocks and the appearance of limestone on the surface. This can be seen very clearly at Settle, with Castleberg Hill, a white limestone crag, perched high above the town. Just north of Stainforth the North Craven Fault brings to the surface the extremely old Silurian Slates which extend just beyond Horton-in-Ribblesdale. These slates are quarried extensively near Helwith Bridge and are easily seen from the Way when descending Moor Head Lane to Helwith Bridge. Great Scar Limestone lies on top of these rocks and can be seen at the very top of the workings, unquarried.

Just beyond Horton-in-Ribblesdale the walker has made enough height - and the tilt of the strata favours him - to walk upon the limestone pastures, well drained and giving delightful walking. Here are the caves and potholes of Sell Gill, Calf Holes, Birkwith, all close to the Way. Caves and potholes are a special feature of the Great Scar Limestone, and are formed by water action on the rock. Beyond Nether Lodge the limestone is covered with a thick layer of boulder clay left by the retreating glaciers of the last Ice Age, some 8,000 years ago. For the first time along the route glaciation has played a more important part in the forming of the landscape than rock types. This is partly because the Ribble Valley did not have a large glacier as many of the dales did. The greater flow of ice from the Irish Sea reduced its size, but at the valley head it left its mark in a whole series of drumlins, slightly elongated mounds of glacial debris left by the retreating ice. The Way goes round about and up and down them until it reaches Gearstones. At Thorns Gill, indeed

A typical riverside path along the Ribble Way. Photo: R.B.Evans

at the other gills of Ribblesdale, the water has carved through the boulder clay and other debris to reach and cut into the limestone and form a little gorge.

Beyond Thorns Gill the rock strata change to those of the Yoredale Series. These are narrow bands of limestone, sandstone and shale and at this altitude give poorly drained land that will only grow the coarse grass and rushes that predominate almost to the very end. Here, as it happens, one of the narrow bands of Yoredale Limestone caps Gayle Wold and it produces the verdant greens so different from the rest of the moor. Indeed, it is the junction between the limestone band and the impervious sandstone band below it that causes the springs that are the source of the Ribble.

With such a varied geological background one could expect a wide range of plant species. This is only true up to a point, for there are a number of factors that tend to override the effect of differing rock types. These are climate, the covering of boulder clay, the alluvial soils of the river's flood plain and man's many activities - farming, forestry, even walking.

The flowers the walker will see are mainly those of the woodland, the hedgerows, and the wet places, where they are neither grazed

The way passes through Avenham Park, Preston
The River Ribble at Preston. Photos : Richard Lowe

The Ribble valley from the Way above Hothersall Hall.
Photo: Aileen Evans

nor trampled nor picked. Efficient farming methods mean that all our old meadow land, once rich with flowers, has been ploughed out and the land re-seeded with rye grass and clover mixtures. They are easy to spot - dull deep green fields compared with the paler green of the native hedge banks. Many wet places are in the woodland, for the farmer drains his productive fields, and woodlands, particularly those in deep cut valleys, tend to be left to themselves. One such place is Tun Brook Wood, full of shade- and moisture-loving plants that thrive in humus-rich soils. The vegetation of the Rainber Scar woodland is completely different. Here the rock is Chatburn Limestone which produces a soil containing more lime than those derived from gritstones and sandstones, and the commonest tree is the hazel, hardly found in woodland lower down the valley, with a little elm, ash, sycamore and oak. Most of the woodland in the lower valley is a mixture of oak, beech, sycamore, elm, hawthorn, and, just occasionally, ash. Again, vast stretches of Rainber woods support only one or two species of shade-loving plants on the ground beneath the trees, for example, wild garlic or dog's mercury, whereas the ground flora of Tun Brook Wood is particularly varied. In Rainber woods there are islands of ungrazed grass which support a rather different collection of plants. There are primroses, great glorious banks of them, patches of speedwell turn the grass blue by the river, and just here and there, the early purple orchid, almost too exotic looking to be true. Long may they remain to give pleasure to the walkers of the Way so, do your bit, look, but do not pick.

The plant population reverts to the norm beyond these woods and not until Upper Ribblesdale is reached will the walker find any marked changes. The reasons are man's grazing animals and the lack of woodland and hedgerows for this is stone wall country. Very occasionally the bird's eye primrose may be found in the wet limestone pastures and the mountain pansy in the uplands above the valley floor. At Nether Lodge the walker leaves the limestone pastures and crosses first the drumlins and then the moors at the foot of the Pennine ridges. Here the underlying rock structures and the boulder clay give badly drained acid soils. There are few flowers to delight the eye: coarse dull green-brown grasses and rushes dominate the landscape, only a stunted hawthorn or two in sight, for here the land is 1,000 feet and more above sea level, too high for tree growth. Yet at the end, the very end, at the spring that is the source of the Ribble, there is another change. The spring burbles out at the foot of a little limestone crag and here in July the grass is truly green and there are flowers, tiny buttercups, brooklime, scurvy grass, thyme, all in startling contrast with the dull moor around. A fine finish for the botanically minded!

Just as plants are very selective in their habitats, so are birds, largely because of their different food requirements. Birds, like flowers, are seasonal, best seen in springtime unless they are winter migrants. In spring and early summer the most striking bird to be seen on the marshes is the shelduck. A large black and white bird, with a chestnut band on the chest of the male, it flies with the head and tail held low, and only seen from late winter to early July as it emigrates after nesting. Though commonest on the mud flats where it feeds, the occasional pair may be seen as far inland as Gisburn. Heron may often be seen anywhere along the river, even at Penwortham Bridge, the kingfisher is reputed to be seen from time to time. Water hens and coots may be seen punting along in the quiet pools in many places. Mallard are common enough along the river in springtime, so too, are black-headed gulls, oystercatchers and plovers, all looking for nesting sites. In winter Canada geese arrive to keep the resident gulls company. Small flocks may often be seen on the river where it runs through pasture, for geese are grass eaters.

In springtime on the marshlands the air is vibrant with the song of skylarks, the woodlands resound with the song of small birds. In almost any of them the walkers may hear the metallic 'honk-honk' of the pheasant or the gentle cooing of the wood pigeon. More than likely the walker will be surprised by the noisy vigorous flappings of wings from time to time of these self-same birds. Beyond Gisburn there is a subtle change in the countryside. The transition is slow but by degrees the birds of the woodlands disappear and those of the rough pastures and the moorland take their place. There is the curlew with its descending warbling trill, the peewit or lapwing, plovers, occasionally the snipe. These moorland birds preponderate right to the source, but in winter hard weather drives them to the marshes to find food and they only return in the spring. The arrival of the curlew is a sure sign of the return of spring to the moors.

One could hardly describe the face of Ribblesdale without mentioning salmon: the Ribble has been famous for its salmon for centuries. Fishing rights on the river are controlled by the North West Water Authority and a licence from them is required to fish. Fishing rights are also the property of the landowner and stretches of the river are let out to a number of angling clubs, for salmon is prized as a 'sporting' fish and commands a high price in the market. The salmon has a most unusual life cycle. It hatches in the gravel beds of the upland tributaries in early spring and spends the first three years of its life in the river. On reaching maturity it goes to sea and after a variable length of time returns in the autumn to spawn. Great numbers of fish swim up the river from the end of September to the beginning of December and this is the best time of year to look out for them wherever there is an obstacle such as a weir or a small waterfall to be passed. Salmon have quite remarkable powers of leaping and swimming up chutes of water. During the time when the fish are 'running' as this annual migration is called, they do not eat, consequently after spawning in January they are very thin and unfit to eat, so this is the close season for salmon fishing. Many of these weakened fish die and may be found on the river banks, partly eaten. This is usually the work of mink, escaped from fur farms, as the otter is now very scarce on the Ribble.

With fertile soils that would bear good crops of corn, a productive river, rich in pastures, sufficient woodland and good building stone it is hardly surprising that in medieval times the lower valley could support a Norman castle, two abbeys and two of their granges as well as a large number of fine halls of residence belonging to the local gentry. Some of these remain today - Samlesbury, Alton, Hothersall, Osbaldeston, Dinckley, Stonyhurst, Little Mitton, Great Mitton, Hacking, Waddow and Gisburn are probably the best known, and have become part of our architectural heritage. The Industrial Revolution touched Ribblesdale but lightly. The Leeds and Liverpool canal's original route would have brought it into the Ribble Valley near Balderstone and taken it out at Whalley but in fact the canal was built via Blackburn and Burnley. The coal and cotton it brought helped to establish early industry there on a large scale. The railway came rather late into the Ribble Valley - it was 1850 before the Blackburn-Chatburn line was opened by the

Lancashire and Yorkshire Railway Company and as it was only a branch line ending at Chatburn it did not bring the good communications that enabled Preston to develop so rapidly. For these two reasons the Ribble Valley escaped the despoilation that the Industrial Revolution brought to so much of the Lancashire countryside.

Above Paythorne the wide marshy expanse of the river flood plain is good for nothing but rough grazing and wild fowl. There was once a proposal to build a reservoir there but nothing came of it. Beyond Settle the river is in an upland environment. Horton-in-Ribblesdale, for example, is 800 feet above sea level. Here the climate is appreciably harsher and were it not for the well drained limestone soils the entire valley would be unproductive moorland. In past times its remoteness and climate made life that little bit harder for man and it was never nearly so well populated as the lower valley. Today the lack of woodland, grey stone walls instead of fences and the background of the peaks of Ingleborough and Pen-y-ghent make a splendid contrast with the lushness of the lower valley.

BEFORE YOU START

In this guidebook the Ribble Way has been divided rather arbitrarily into sections related to major roads with public transport to help those people who wish to do the Way or part of it as a series of day trips. Cheap accommodation is lacking for most of the Way and the campsites are scarce.

The Paths

During 1984-5 Lancashire County Council did the work needed to convert a collection of often neglected right of way footpaths and short stretches of road into this new recreational footpath where it lies within the county. In addition a number of new right of way paths were created, some to legalise paths habitually used by the public without that right, others to link or modify existing paths. Improvements were made to a few stretches of path, many stiles and footbridges over the frequent streams and ditches were built.

Walkers should note that there are many other footpaths, particularly by the river. These are anglers' concessionary paths, not rights of way, and although they look attractive, they must not be used. Waymarking has been done, but it is rather erratic. Within the Yorkshire Dales National Park the logo will only be found on existing signposts. There is scope for the walker to use his/her skills interpreting map and guidebook.

Maps

The maps included in this book should make the walker independent of any other map purely for route-finding purposes and the 1:25,000 Pathfinder Series of maps is hardly necessary. However, the 1:25,000 Yorkshire Dales Outdoor Leisure Maps Nos.2 and 10 which cover the Way from Wigglesworth to the source of the Ribble are necessary, for waymarking in Yorkshire is sometimes sparse and the route is not well trodden. In the 1:50,000 Landranger Series of maps sheet nos.102, 103 and 98 cover the entire Way and enable the walker to plan his/her route as well as giving a useful picture of the Ribble Valley.

Equipment

No special clothing or equipment is needed, though it is worth remembering the old couplet:

Hodder, Calder, Ribble and rain
All come together in Mitton domaine

Overtrousers are particularly useful when passing through hayfields after rain. Despite the improvements to drainage and surface of some paths there are still a number of wet places, some caused by springs and streamlets in the woodlands, others, far more obnoxious, are caused by cattle churning the ground in wet weather. As the walker must live with these, lightweight boots are recommended as the right footwear in all but the driest weather.

Facilities

A list of facilities available in the towns and villages on or close to the Way is given at the start of each section. Places for refreshment are particularly important as the lower Ribble Valley is a countryside of fences and hedges offering little shelter for lunch breaks in bad weather.

Transport

There have been many changes to the bus and train services in the Ribble Valley since the first edition of this book. Lancashire County Council has now tourist information centres in the following Lancashire towns and a visit to one of them would resolve most of your transport queries: Accrington, Blackburn, Blackpool, Burnley, Chorley, Fleetwood, Lancaster, Leyland, Lytham, Morecambe, Nelson, Ormskirk, Preston, Rawtenstall, Skelmersdale. Look in your local telephone directory to find the relevant address. If this is inconvenient ring the county's transport enquiry line for bus services: 0772 263333. It will however, make the job easier if you are aware of the possibilities (as they were in the summer of 1991) before you enquire.

There is a good bus service between Preston and The Rams, Longton, and some buses go on to Southport passing the Golden Ball, considerably nearer to The Dolphin than The Rams. On Sundays only there is a through service between Liverpool and Blackpool that goes through Longton. Where the Way crosses the A6 at Walton-le-Dale there are fairly frequent buses to Chorley and Bolton and some to Wigan. The next major road crossed, the A59, is on a bus route to Blackburn. Ribchester, at the end of the next section is on another (2-hourly) Preston-Blackburn route which travels via Grimsargh. It is worth noting that Grimsargh taps the much more frequent Longridge-Preston service and can be a better finishing point to the day than Ribchester. Clitheroe has a service to Preston that runs via Edisford Bridge and Hurst Green NOT Ribchester, and there is no bus service between these two places. Clitheroe is also served by the Skipton-Preston bus which stops at Gisburn, and in the reverse direction is potentially useful to Yorkshire folk. There is a good service from Clitheroe to Blackburn via Whalley. All these Clitheroe buses start at Well Terrace which is much nearer to Brungerley Bridge than to Edisford Bridge.

Getting back to Lancashire from Settle and places beyond is not easy. There are two possibilities: the bus to Skipton (hourly) then the Skipton-Preston bus or the Skipton-Burnley via Earby bus, depending where you live, or the train. Giggleswick Station is on the Leeds-Morecambe line with six trains a day stopping at Lancaster. The station is a short mile from where the Way crosses Penny Lane on the outskirts of Settle. A glance at the Yorkshire Dales Outdoor Leisure Map No.10 makes the route clear. Obviously it is possible to return to Skipton by train from Giggleswick. As the Settle-Carlisle railway has now been restored it is possible to return from Ribblehead Station. In addition Horton has a bus service to Settle run by Whaites Coaches. Their timetable is displayed outside the Peny-y-ghent cafe, that haven for weary walkers, at Horton. To get an update on these facilities, ring the Settle Tourist Information Office: 0729 825192.

Many people will prefer to use a car for part of their journey and possible parking places are given in the Facts and Facilities section at the start of each chapter. Where bus services are infrequent it can be a useful ploy to leave the car at the end of the day's walk and to take a morning bus to the starting point of the day, but note the lack of buses between Clitheroe and Ribchester.

Accommodation

Walkers are warned that there is no cheap accommodation along the Way until Yorkshire is reached. The first (and last) youth hostel is at Stainforth (on the main road south of the village) and there is a Dales Barn at Horton-in-Ribblesdale. This is at Dub Cote Farm, a long uphill mile out of Horton on the lower slopes of Pen-y-ghent, and is marked on the Yorkshire Dales Outdoor Leisure Map No.2. Dales Barns are traditional field barns converted into simple but comfortable self-catering accommodation for walkers. Bunks, cooking, washing and drying facilities are provided but a sheet sleeping bag and pillow case are needed. It is necessary to book in advance. Write or ring Mrs J.Glasgow, Dub Cote Farm, Horton-in-Ribblesdale, Settle, BD24 0ET, (07296 238). The Dales Barn at Cam Houses is very close to the end of the Way and it could be useful to stay the night there before a return from Ribblehead Station. Contact Mrs D.Smith, Cam Houses, Upper Langstrothdale, Near Outershaw, Buckden, Skipton, BD23 5JT, (0860 648045).

It is worth knowing that the Yorkshire Dales National Park Committee sell an accommodation guide to the Park that costs around 50p. It covers campsites, bunkhouse barns and bed and breakfast accommodation. Write to them at Colvend, Hebden Road, Grassington, Skipton, BD23 5LB.

Otherwise the walker must stay in pubs, farmhouses or guest houses. In Preston there is a cluster of inexpensive hotels on Fishergate Hill, in Stanley Place and Stanley Terrace, all 5 minutes walk from the railway station and the bus stop to Longton, and less than 10 minutes from where the Way enters Broadgate at the bottom of Fishergate Hill. Preston Tourist Information Office, Lancaster Road, Preston, (0772 53731) offers a free booklet, *Where to Stay and Eat in Preston* that lists them all. Ribble Valley Borough Council, Council Offices, Church Walk, Clitheroe, (0200 255111) offer a similar one that covers the Ribble Valley from Ribchester to Gisburn. Settle Tourist Information Office, Council Offices, Victoria Street, Settle, (07292 5192) offers information from Rathmell to Horton in Ribblesale during the summer. At Horton itself the Pen-y-ghent cafe doubles as a tourist information office and will help in finding accommodation (07296 333).

Campsites

Campsites are scarce too and most caravan sites do not take tents. There is a good campsite at Edisford Bridge, Clitheroe and another at Todber Caravan Park, Gisburn (well off route, $1^1/2$ miles up the hill on the A682 to Nelson) and that is all in the Lancashire part of the Way. In Yorkshire the first campsite is at Knight Stainforth and the Way passes through it. It has good facilities and a shop. Holm Farm, Horton-in-Ribblesdale, opposite the church, now has a campsite with basic facilities. There are many delightful spots along the Way, but permission to camp must always be sought before actually doing so, and no stream can be regarded as safe to drink.

Last but not least

Some stiles around Helwith Bridge carry a sticker, 'Country landowners welcome careful walkers'. An admirable statement. Careful walkers will always:

1. Take all their rubbish with them.
2. Be careful with matches, cigarettes and stoves.
3. Close all gates, including difficult ones, so that animals cannot stray.
4. Keep their dog on a lead at all times.
5. Walk in a single file in hay fields.
6. Take care not to pollute streams.
7. Enjoy flowers where they are growing.

EXPLANATION of

Large Scale Strip Maps

_____ PUBLIC ROAD

___ PRIVATE DRIVE OR FARM TRACK

_____ UNFENCED ROAD, TRACK

_____ ROAD or TRACK USED BY 〰

_____ PATH USED BY 〰

_____ OTHER PATH

_____ BUILDINGS

__ OUTLINE OF TOWN OR VILLAGE

_____ CHURCH, CHAPEL

_____ WALL, HEDGE OR FENCE

_____ EMBANKMENT

__ESCARPMENT (If space permits)

_____ CAMPING SITE, PUB

_____ RIVER, STREAM

___ROAD BRIDGE, FOOT BRIDGE

_____ WOODLAND & BUSHES

_____PINES

Section 1
LONGTON TO PENWORTHAM BRIDGE, PRESTON

Facts and facilities

Mileage: 7.0

Map: 1:50,000 Landranger Series Sheet No.102 Preston and Blackpool

At Longton

Toilets: in a side street almost opposite The Rams

Pubs: The Rams, the Golden Ball and The Dolphin

Café/Shops/P.O./Telephone: all in a block of shops opposite the church and close to The Rams

Bus Stop: most buses from Preston stop at The Rams, not the Golden Ball

Parking: no public car park. Not possible at the start of Marsh Lane

The route

Originally the Way started at the Golden Ball which is at the junction of Liverpool Road and Marsh Lane, though the real walking does not start until the end of that lane at The Dolphin, a tiny pub known locally as The Fish. Unless you have a transport manager you will have to walk from The Rams in the centre of Longton which puts a good 1^{1}/$_{2}$ miles on to the day. Simply continue down Liverpool Road to the Golden Ball and turn off into Marsh Lane. Follow it to its end taking the right-hand fork and go straight ahead over the stile onto the marsh bank.[1]

The transition from the landscape of modern suburbia to the wide skies of the marshes was completed in the last few strides. The scene has gradually become more rural and the landscape noticeably flatter. On the marsh bank you enter another world, a tide-washed world. On a good spring day the air is vibrant with the song of skylarks, no sound of man's works penetrate, all are swept away by the ever-present wind. The Ribble is not yet in sight, the narrow slit of river seen over the salt marsh is its final tributary, the Douglas.

27

The Preston Skyline

Turn right on the marsh bank and walk this boundary between sea and land to Longton Brook. As you approach the obvious bridge keep a look out for a stile through the hedge straight ahead. Then turn left and follow the hedge to a stile in about 50 yards. In the lane go left over a stile by the gate, cross the footbridge, and go right over a ladder stile into the cornfield on the edge of the brook. Go through this long field, cross the farm lane and then go the length of another field to rejoin the marsh bank. In due course it makes a big swinging right-hand curve and you find yourself on the bank of the Ribble itself.[2,3]

If the tide is out you will be surprised at the smallness of the river, a mere streamlet in comparison with the enormous width of the river bed on the bank of which you will walk for the next 4 miles or so. Preston lies ahead, identified only by the white needle-like spire of St Walburg's Church.[4] You

*will gradually zoom in on this in slow, slow, motion, until the industrial
sprawl blots out the distant view of the Bowlands and the West Pennine
Moors, and the spire is framed by a forest of electricity pylons.*

In due course cross Mill Brook by a good bridge.[5] Now the wide
grassy bank becomes much smaller and there are many little paths.
They all go the same way, just take care not to leave the bank.[6]
Eventually you will find yourself on a cart track that leads to a
transformer station on the site of the former electricity works. Here
you join a tarmac road that passes through a pleasantly landscaped
area with a grassed and mown strip that gives some relief to the feet.
Follow it all the way to the A59 at Penwortham Bridge.[7]

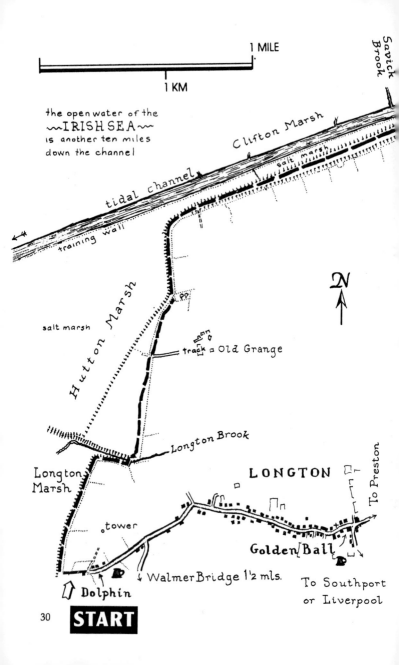

1 MILE

1 KM

the open water of the
~IRISH SEA~
is another ten miles
down the channel

Savick Brook

Clifton Marsh

salt marsh

tidal channel

training wall

Hutton Marsh

salt marsh

N

track ⊐ Old Grange

Longton Brook

LONGTON

Longton
Marsh

To Preston

.tower

Golden Ball

To Southport
or Liverpool

⇨ Dolphin

↓ Walmer Bridge 1½ mls.

30 **START**

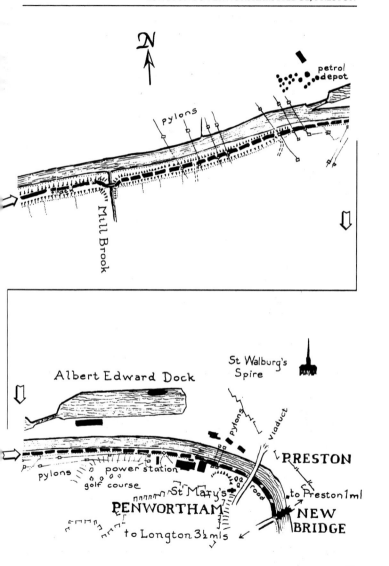

N

petrol depot

pylons

Track

Mill Brook

Albert Edward Dock

St Walburg's Spire

pylons

viaduct

PRESTON

pylons

power station

golf course

St Mary's

PENWORTHAM

road

to Preston 1 ml

NEW BRIDGE

to Longton 3½ mls

Things seen along the Way

1.   Longton is a place of fairly ancient origin; though not as old as Preston. It was probably established in the middle of the twelfth century, but today no trace of its ancient origin remains: it is a piece of modern suburbia. The Ribble marshes have been progressively enclosed and the land reclaimed by building earth banks for centuries. The remains of an old bank can be seen running across the fields from The Dolphin to Longton Brook. The one used by the Way was probably built in the 1850s. In the late 1830s The Dolphin was a private house with a garden belonging to a local brewer. It seems reasonable to assume that when the marsh banks were being built the house started to sell beer and became a pub. It is known to have been a pub since 1881.

2.   As you are walking the broad bank of the Ribble you will quite frequently see stout posts with chains or cables attached to them. When the port of Preston was in regular use the river had to be kept clear of silt and sand by dredgers. They tied up to these posts whilst they were working and deposited their loads on the opposite banks forming the huge piles of sand and gravel there.

3.   If you are doing the Way in springtime, you will almost certainly see shelduck in this same part of the Ribble, for its silt beds are their feeding grounds. They are large, quite striking birds, black and white with a chestnut band on the chest of the males, though this can only be seen fairly close to. They fly in a characteristic head and tail down position. After they have nested they emigrate and only return in the spring. With luck you may see cormorants and an occasional heron.

4.   St. Walburg's Church might be thought to be some magnificent medieval building, but in fact was built in 1850-54, the time when Preston's population was increasing rapidly. Its steeple is the top part of a four-stage tower and the whole is 300 feet high.

5.   The marshes themselves are almost devoid of flowers, for they are too heavily grazed, but the bridge at Mill Brook cuts them off from the banks beyond and flowering plants are now found. In the wet banks of Mill Brook you will see in early May an uncommon plant called scurvy grass. It is not a grass but a remote member of the cabbage family. Further along you may find sweet cicily, a plant

The river at Dinkley.
Cromwell's Bridge. Photos: R.B.Evans

Mitton
Hacking Hall and the confluence of the Calder
Photos: R.B.Evans

common to the Yorkshire Dales, for it likes a limestone soil. In August and September some stretches are yellow with common ragwort, a plant which is poisonous to animals and therefore not eaten by them. You will even see what appears to be a giant ragwort, towering 5 feet high. This is saracen's woundwort, an uncommon plant.

6. Oil tanks become sadly prominent on the opposite bank: just past them is the entrance to the Albert Edward Dock, opened in 1892 and now converted into a marina.

7. Penwortham was one of the most important towns in Lancashire in Norman times. Nothing remains of the Norman town today except the artificial mound of Castle Hill where the motte and bailey castle was built to guard the ford across the river at this point.

*   *   *

Section 2

PENWORTHAM BRIDGE TO BROCKHOLES BRIDGE, PRESTON

Facts and facilities

Mileage: 5.0

Map: 1:50,000 Landranger Series Sheet No.102 Preston and Blackpool

Pubs: one at the start of Broadgate, another at the entrance to Miller Park, another at Walton Bridge

Cafés: chip shop at the start of Broadgate

Shops: at the start of Broadgate and on Fishergate Hill. Early closing day Thursday

P.O.:   at the start of Broadgate

Telephone: at the start of Broadgate

Bus Stop: at the bottom of Fishergate Hill for buses both into Preston and to Longton

Parking: in Broadgate itself, in the lane by the Shawes Arms at Walton Bridge. Very limited parking in a lay-by on the south side of Brockholes Bridge. Usually full

The route

Turn left to cross the bridge and cross the Liverpool-Preston road at the traffic lights - much safer. Broadgate lies straight ahead and you follow this pleasant tree-lined street on the very banks of the Ribble[1] until it ends in a gravel road just before the railway arches. Strangely, the scene is almost rural again, quiet, grassy and inviting after the turmoil of Liverpool Road. The Way goes under the railway arches[2] to enter Miller Park and follows a pleasant riverside path into Avenham Park,[3,4] then into Frenchwood Recreation Ground. This path ends in Ashworth Grove, and from here a well situated path follows the river bank right to Walton Bridge[5] on the A6.

Cross the A6, here dual carriageway and not too difficult, to the Shawes Arms. Go down the right-hand side of the pub and follow the lane until it forks. On the right you will see a stile leading to the riverside path which gives excellent walking right to the wood.

Here the Ribble slowly meanders across its flood plain between the bluffs on which Higher Walton Church stands and those clothed by Red Scar Woods. You may get your first glimpse of Pendle Hill, which, though it can scarcely be said to dominate the Ribble Valley, occurs time and again in the views. Swallows and martins quarter the river for midges - and there is often a goodly supply. Black-headed gulls and oystercatchers, usually thought of as sea birds, still frequent this stretch of river, for it is tidal almost to Brockholes Bridge but there are too many grazing animals to have a chance of seeing more than the odd daisy until you come to the wood.

Enter the wood by a stile close to the river and follow the little path until it reaches a raised concrete pipe whose broad, flat top makes an excellent path as it snakes its way through the impenetrable undergrowth of the wood. When you emerge into the open air, turn

Penwortham Old Bridge

right to reach the river bank once more and follow it to the Brockholes Bridge,[7] the A59 again.

The Way now goes under the flood arch to spare you the considerable hazards of crossing the busy road. It appears blocked but there is a gap at the left-hand end and a few yards of newly created path leads you to the farm access road - and to Section 3.

Note
If you want to go into Preston do not use this underpass, but instead follow the path to the left and up to the road, where there is a footpath up Brockholes Brow to the bus stop at the top. If you want to go to Blackburn, use it, for the bus stop is on the far side of the second roundabout.

Things seen on the Way

About Preston
Strictly speaking Preston is only the town on the north side of the Ribble, for that is where it was founded, possibly in the seventh century. Very little is known of that period and not a great deal

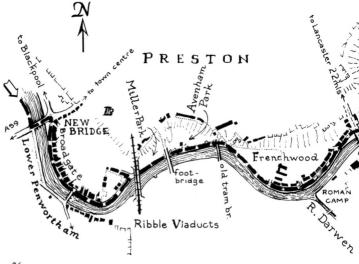

about the town or village as it was then, in medieval times. However, the structures that may interest walkers of the Ribble Way were all built much later when, thanks to the Industrial Revolution, Preston had grown enormously and become an industrial town. It may fairly be said that Richard Arkwright, born in Preston in 1732, was the father of the Industrial Revolution in Lancashire, for in 1770 he invented the spinning or water frame, a machine that, by using power from a water-wheel, enabled cotton to be spun into yarn far faster than could be done by hand. Arkwright House has been restored and Stoneygate, where it is situated, is easily reached from Avenham Park. Although Arkwright did not exploit his invention in Preston, the town became a major producer of cotton goods and had all the services associated with trade and industry. The following structures passed on the Way are all associated with this period of Preston's history.

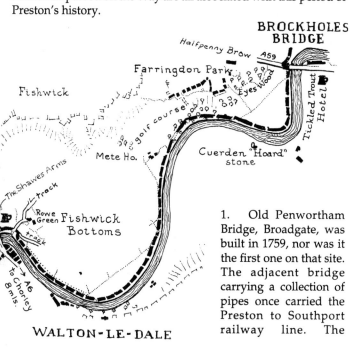

1. Old Penwortham Bridge, Broadgate, was built in 1759, nor was it the first one on that site. The adjacent bridge carrying a collection of pipes once carried the Preston to Southport railway line. The

embankment can be seen quite clearly on the other side of the river.

2.   The Preston-Wigan railway was built in 1838 and the line to east Lancashire in 1850. The two separate railway companies involved built the two bridges in Miller Park.

3.   Avenham Park was established by the Corporation during the period 1861-7 in what had been a market garden area. Avenham Walk, leading to it, had been established as a leisure area and planted with trees as early as 1696.

4.   The Tramway Bridge in Avenham Park is a relic of the Lancaster Canal, devised to enable Lancaster and Kendal to develop in the way that towns further south were doing in the late eighteenth century. There was a vastly increased demand for coal especially in the Preston area where the cotton industry was growing fast. Because the roads were so bad coal was generally brought from Wigan by boat down the River Douglas, dependent on tides and winds, and canal transport was much cheaper. (See *The Douglas Valley Way* by Gladys Sellers, Cicerone Press.) The canal was started at both ends simultaneously but the proposed crossing of the Ribble Valley by a staircase of locks and an aqueduct proved to be far too expensive, and the much cheaper expedient of two tram roads linked by a bridge was adopted. The tree-lined embankment of the tram road leading to the terminus of the southern part at Johnson's Hillock can be seen across the river. The stationary steam engine for that side was at Walton-le-Dale, that for the Preston side was housed in the white porticoed building at the top of the hill above the bridge. The present steel bridge was built in 1860, the first one built of wood in 1802. From the pump house on the north side, the tramway went along the top of the park below the houses, turned right, went along what is now the Asda car park and through the tunnel that goes into Corporation Street to the basin at the terminus of the northern end.

5.   There has been a bridge at Walton-le-Dale since 1403. Traces of its embutments can be seen downstream of the present bridge built in 1782 and doubled in width during World War II.

6.   As you are walking along the banks of the Ribble well beyond Higher Walton Church you will notice a solitary brick house across

the river. Not far from it the Cuerdale Hoard was discovered by workmen in the banks of the river in 1840. This hoard was a huge collection of around 10,000 early silver coins and a considerable weight of silver ingots. The coins were Scandinavian and were minted between AD 815 and 930. It is thought that the hoard may have belonged to a Danish army as it is too big to have belonged to an individual. It is a matter of conjecture whether the chest was buried whilst the army was in flight or lost in an attempt to cross the river. A stone marks the site, but there is no public access to it.

7. Brockholes Bridge was rebuilt in 1824 when the Preston-Blackburn turnpike road was being constructed. It is called Halfpenny Bridge locally, for a halfpenny was the cost of the toll. This bridge was swept away by floods in August 1840 and today's bridge built in 1861.

✳   ✳   ✳

The Old Tram Bridge. Winter Hill is seen in the distance

Section 3
BROCKHOLES BRIDGE TO RIBCHESTER

Facts and facilities

Mileage: 9.5

Map: 1:50,000 Landranger Series Sheet No.102 Preston and Blackpool

At Ribchester

Toilets: on the car park, well signposted

Pubs: three

Cafés: tea, cake and ice-cream only in summer, in Water Street

Shops: all kinds on the main street. Early closing day Wednesday

P.O.:   in the main street.

Telephone: 100 yards from the P.O.

Parking: free car park, well signposted

The route

When you reach Lower Brockholes Farm, a pleasant building that has evidently seen many alterations and additions, bear right along a wide gravel road. Follow it under the motorway, then take the right-hand fork, which eventually becomes grassy - avoid going off into the fields for the Way is always between hedges. There are several iron gates across it close to the site of Higher Brockholes Hall, now no more than a collection of thistle-grown humps and bumps on the left of the track. At the last gate follow the fence (made of motorway crash barriers!) to the left to enter Red Scar Wood. Climb steadily upwards on a good path, and at the top bear right on a cinder track that runs round the edge of playing fields. At a T-junction turn right passing a brick tower on its right to reach a well-made path that runs along the top edge of the wood. Follow it for half a mile or so to the point where it is blocked, and here cross the

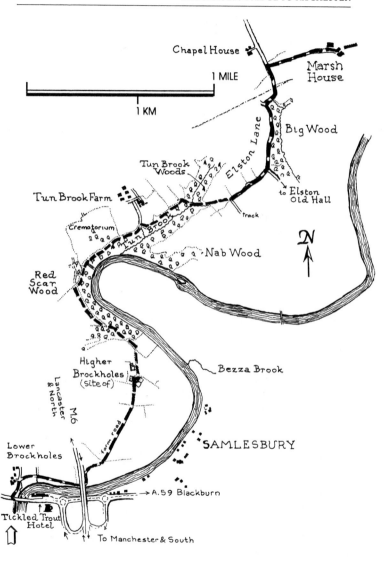

stile into the field. Now bear left keeping parallel to the wood, cross
three smallish fields, then cut across the corner of the fourth field to
enter Tun Brook Wood, which, together with Red Scar Wood, is a
Nature Reserve managed by the Lancashire Trust for Nature
Conservation.[1] The descent into the wood is steep, aided by
crumbling steps and a handrail, but thankfully the ascent is much
less demanding.

*Tun Brook Wood is substantial enough to act as a barrier to the urban
atmosphere - the views of industrial buildings, noise, litter and rubbish
around, that marks much of the Way up to this point. Ahead lies the Ribble
Valley, rural and unspoilt except for a short stretch around Clitheroe. As
you walk along Elston Lane, delightfully quiet, shaded by oak trees and
fringed with cow parsley in early summer, you are walking along a shelf
on the edge of the valley. The river is down below, making a distant
meander. Beyond it you may see the West Pennine Moors identified by*

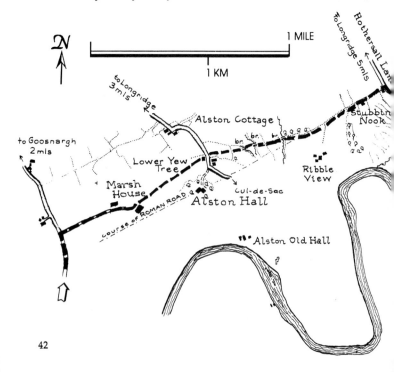

Darwen Tower. Great Hill lies to its right, Hoghton Tower is on the nearer wooded hillock that lies between them. Pendle Hill is not yet in sight, only the "Little End" above Whalley. When you've turned the sharp corner in the lane, part of the Bowlands behind Chipping come into view. Parlick is the lower hill, and behind it, Fairsnape Fell.

When you emerge from the wood make diagonally right to find the stile by the gate into Elston Lane. Turn left and follow this lane for almost a mile, bearing left at the first junction, until you come to a gated lane on the right with a prominent waymark and a finger post "Footpath to Hothersall Lane ¾ mile". Beyond the house, Marsh Farm, follow the lane to its end then enter the field at a stone stile. Follow the hedge in the first field then cut across the next large field to reach Alston Lane just to the left of the cottages. Go straight across the lane into a large field, and, keeping just to the left of the

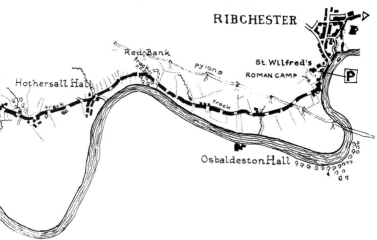

line of electricity poles, drop steeply down the bank to find the first of three partly hidden footbridges. The others lie straight ahead. After the last one make your way steeply up the hillside to the right of the wood. Follow the hedge to Stubbins Nook and thence to Hothersall Lane.

Turn right down the lane and follow it down the hill to its end at Hothersall Hall.[2] Go left past the front of the hall and up the gravel

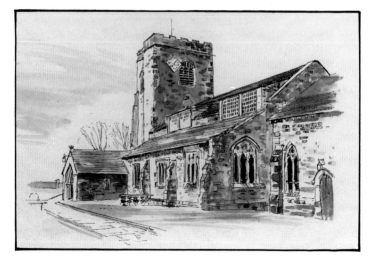

Ribchester Church

road to where it swings left. Here go over the stile by the gate on the right aiming for the top of the wood and then follow its edge all the way down to the riverbank. Again, there have been tantalising glimpses of the river from the road, but here, for a brief spell, you are close to the river again. After a couple of fields' lengths you reach the rough lane that brings you all the way to Ribchester,[3] passing the Roman museum and the church on your left. As you stand by the river the school lies straight ahead and the Way goes to its right and bypasses the village by a nondescript riverside path to rejoin the main road close to the New Hotel.

It is a pity, though, to miss such a historic and interesting village, the finest visited by the Way. Take an hour or so to wander round it and then make for the New Hotel which is on the Blackburn road at the east end of the village.

Things seen on the Way

1. If you have an interest in botany and you are doing the Way in spring or early summer, Tun Brook Wood has much of interest. It is sheltered and heavily shaded and, having a richer soil than many of

44

the deep cut cloughs of the West Pennine Moors, has a far bigger variety of both trees and herbaceous plants. You will find wych elm, ash, hazel, bird cherry and guelder rose as well as the ubiquitous oak, sycamore and hawthorn. As you descend the east-facing side which is wetter than the other, you will find golden saxifrage, yellow pimpernel, ground ivy, herb bennett and violets. I'm sure primroses could be found in some remote corner, for primroses are irresistible and soon plundered. There are two particularly interesting plants, not common in Lancashire: sanicle and our biggest sedge, *Carex pendula*. It grows 3 to 4 feet high, its leaves are blade-like, an inch wide, and its flower stalks bear catkin-like heads topped by a thin brownish spike which is the male flower, for sedges bear separate male and female flowers. You may also find this plant in Raisber Wood. At the bottom of the valley there is a patch of sweet woodruffe and harts tongue ferns hidden away. The upper part of the opposite side is drier than the rest, parts of it are carpeted with wood anemone, but you will also find celandine, lords and ladies, oxalis, germander speedwell, and dog's mercury and enchanters' nightshade, two not very interesting plants to look at. The first of them is only found in ancient woodland or hedges that are the remains of woodland. It seems probable that Tun Brook Wood has always been woodland, but this does not mean it has not been cut and replanted many times.

2. Just before Hothersall Hall comes into sight there is a collection of very modern buildings on the right. This is the Lancashire County Council's Field Studies Centre, where schoolchildren do the practical work for their A-level geography and botany. Hothersall Hall itself, like all the halls of the Ribble Valley is on the site of a much older one. The present structure was built just before World War I, and farms much of the land around. In the fields round here you may see cows wearing collars with coloured plastic boxes. These boxes contain computerised information that controls the amount of supplementary rations fed to each cow according to its milk output. That's modern farming for you!

3. Osbaldeston Hall is well seen across the river during the last half mile to Ribchester. Like Hacking Hall, still to come, it has a number of gables but it is not so fine. Again, like Hacking Hall - and a great many more houses in the area it was rebuilt in the early part of the

seventeenth century and had its own ferry.

Ribchester

Ribchester's attractiveness arises from its rows of neat cottages and houses, relics of the eighteenth and nineteenth century weaving industry rather than from its Roman remains of which disappointingly little can be seen. Some of them lie beneath the churchyard and adjacent houses - part of the rampart can be seen just outside the west gate of the churchyard. After the Roman fort was abandoned it was used as a source of ready-cut stone for all sorts of later buildings. The pillars of the porch of the White Bull are reputed to have come from the fort, those of the singing gallery of the church may have done. The river changed its course in the eighteenth century and washed away the whole of the south-east corner of the fort, not a complete loss to archaeology for the river erosion uncovered the splendid ceremonial helmet and visor in 1786. Probably the best of its kind ever discovered in the British Isles, the original is in the British Museum, that in Ribchester is a copy. The fort, Brementennacum, dates from AD 79, a time when Agricola was advancing northwards against the Brigantes. It was built to guard the river crossing of the road from Manchester to Carlisle and the road to Ilkley and Kirkham. As it safeguarded such important lines of communication it became one of the biggest in Lancashire and was occupied by heavy cavalry from the Danube. When they retired many of these men settled locally making a large civilian settlement around the fort now covered by the village. The museum has a good display of some of the objects that have been excavated and a painting illustrating how people lived at that time. The excavated remains of the granaries can be seen in its yard, but the only others are the remains of the bath house off Greenside. (From the museum go past the White Bull and turn right into Greenside. Then take the first right and the excavation is at the end of the street.)

The Tower of St Wilfred's Church beckons the walker as he/she approaches Ribchester. St Wilfred was Archbishop of York in AD 664 and a great church builder. This does not imply he built Ribchester Church, but it is quite possible he visited it. The first impression of the building, one of interesting bits and pieces, arises

The White Bull, Ribchester

because of the many additions and alterations made over the centuries. The main body of the church was built in the early part of the thirteenth century and has a fine triple lancet window characteristic of that period. It almost certainly incorporates an earlier Norman church - there is a blocked-up Norman doorway in the north wall - which in turn replaced an even earlier one. The porch and Dutton choir are fourteenth-century work though the fine tower was not built until the fifteenth century. Dutton is one of the townships that make up the parish and the Way goes through it. The church contains many features which will appeal to those interested in church architecture. In particular there are the dormer windows, probably put in about the year 1700 to improve the light in the nave, and the Singing Gallery built in 1736 to accommodate musicians. Under the commonwealth's puritanical administration all church organs had been destroyed and after the Restoration in 1660 simpler musical instruments came into use.

Little or nothing is known of the village during the period of time spanned by this church building except that it was pillaged by the Scots in 1332, a not uncommon occurrence in the north of England after the Battle of Bannockburn, and that it was scourged by the Black Death in 1349-50. Probably half of the population died and it took some 300 years before it returned to its former level. Two or three houses of this period remain, including the White Bull. By 1745 Ribchester must have been enjoying some prosperity, for there is a group of fine Georgian houses, brick-built, which is unusual here, but with stone facings. The bulk of the fine stone houses that give Ribchester its character were built somewhat later than that, probably from 1780-1820. Most of them were hand-loom weavers' houses, for at this time, even until the 1830s, hand-loom weaving was the minor occupation of the village. It was carried out in the home, sometimes in cellars lighted by two or three windows at pavement level, sometimes in an upper storey or sometimes in a specially built loomshop at the back of the house. The advent of power looms in the 1840s-50s brought hard times and people moved to the nearby towns to find work, even though there were two textile mills in the village. Today Ribchester is partly dormitory village, and is dependent partly on engineering, and partly on tourism, for it is a most attractive village in a beautiful valley.

For more information see:

Ribchester: A Short History and Guide by A.C.Hodge and J.R.Ridge.

A Goodly Heritage a description of the parish church by J.H.Finch.
The Museum Trust's guide to the Roman period.
These notes are based on the above booklets.

❊ ❊ ❊

*In spring, bluebells carpet the woods
along the Ribble Way. Photo: Richard Lowe*

The Ribble at Paythorne
Cow Bridge, Long Preston. Photos: W.Unsworth

Section 4

RIBCHESTER TO BRUNGERLEY BRIDGE, CLITHEROE

Facts and facilities

Mileage: 11.2

Maps: 1:25,000 Pathfinder Series SD63/73 Great Harwood and Longridge

1:50,000 Landranger Series Sheet No.103 Blackburn and Burnley

At Great Mitton

Toilets: none

Pubs: two

Café/Shop: by the garage, open all the year. Shop with the café

P.O.: none

Telephone: close to the café

Bus Stop: at Mitton Road end, a good mile from the café

Parking: none, but it is possible near the church

At Clitheroe

Toilets: at Edisford Bridge, in Brungerley Park, in the market place

Pubs/Cafés/Shops: Every service in Clitheroe. Early closing day Wednesday. It is $1^{1}/_{2}$ miles from Edisford Bridge, $^{1}/_{2}$ mile from Brungerley Bridge to the town centre

Bus Station: Well Terrace. Note that walkers who wish to return to Preston are on the bus route at Edisford Bridge

Parking: car park and picnic site (not free) at Edisford Bridge. No parking at Brungerley Bridge. Many car parks in Clitheroe

Campsite: at Edisford Bridge

The route

FROM RIBCHESTER TO DINCKLEY FOOTBRIDGE

Follow the main road to the bridge over the river, a short mile. There's a footpath most of the way. (If you want to have a look at Stydd Church[1] and Stydd Almshouses[2] turn left into the lane at Stony Bridge just as you leave the village. The almshouses are on the left about 300 yards ahead and the church is on the right a further 150 yards distant.) At the river bridge go straight ahead along the access road to Dewhurst House. Here turn right in front of the barn and follow the painted arrows to the riverside, to start a fine stretch of pasture and woodland. Follow the banks of the river pulling away briefly as you approach the wood. There are several paths in the wood, it is probably best to keep near the river until you meet a wire fence, then move left to find the stile. Now you climb quite steeply up the hillside, there is no path at present, but no doubt one will appear with use. Keep towards the left and make for the stile by the gate ahead. Shortly after climb up again to the left to the stile at

50

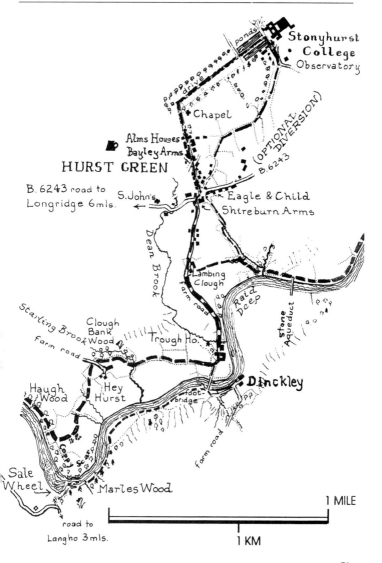

ponds

Stonyhurst College

• Observatory

drive

+ Chapel

(OPTIONAL DIVERSION)

B.6243

Alms Houses
Bayley Arms

HURST GREEN

B. 6243 road to
Longridge 6 mls.

S. John's

Eagle & Child
Shireburn Arms

Dean Brook

Lambing
Clough

farm road

Raid
Deep

stone
Aqueduct

Starling Brook

farm road

Clough
Bank Wood

Trough Ho.

Dinckley

Haugh
Wood

Hey
Hurst

foot-
bridge

farm road

Sale
Wheel

Marles Wood

road to
Langho 3 mls.

1 MILE

1 KM

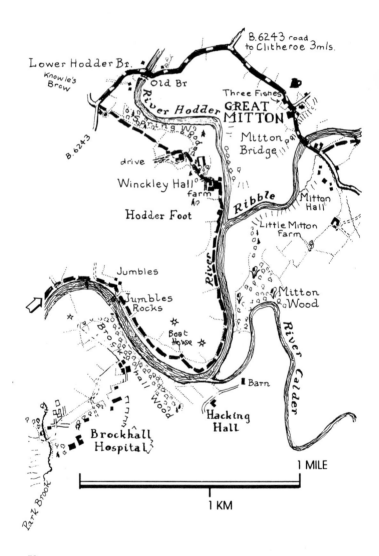

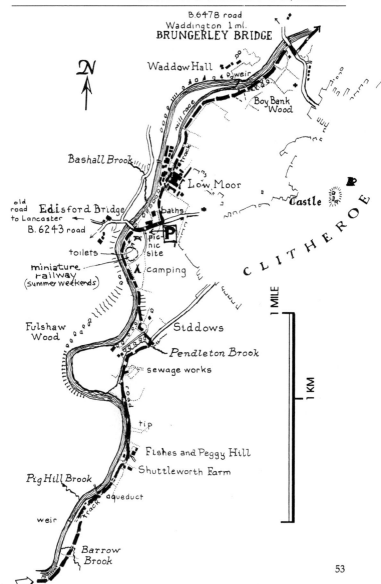

B.6478 road
Waddington 1 ml.
BRUNGERLEY BRIDGE

Waddow Hall

weir

Boy Bank Wood

Bashall Brook

track

mill race

Low Moor

Castle

CLITHEROE

old road to Lancaster ←
B.6243 road

Edisford Bridge

baths

P

pic nic site

toilets

camping

miniature railway (summer weekends)

Fulshaw Wood

Siddows

Pendleton Brook

sewage works

MILE

KM

road

tip

Fishes and Peggy Hill

Shuttleworth Farm

Pig Hill Brook

aqueduct

weir

track

Barrow Brook

53

Stydd Almshouses

the side of the right-hand one of two gates. In the left-hand corner of the field behind Hayhurst Farm you'll find the next stile which puts you onto a farm track, but you cross the stile almost opposite. Now follow the hedge to find the bridge, go straight ahead and again follow the hedge through three fields to reach Trough House, with Dinckley footbridge on the right.

Diversion to Sale Wheel Whirlpool
About ³/₄ mile downstream from Dinckley[3] footbridge is the whirlpool of Sale Wheel, which spins in flood. The right of way path to Sale Wheel passes some of the nicest scenery on the Ribble and is well worth a diversion. Turn right when you have crossed the bridge and follow the riverside path to Sale Wheel, a circular pool past a rocky narrows. Go up towards the road, where the path ends, for the best view of the pool. Then retrace your steps.

DINCKLEY FOOTBRIDGE TO GREAT MITTON

As this book goes to Press changes are due to be made to the route avoiding a tiresome climb up to Hurst Green. As you start this climb look out for a stile on the right as you approach the top of the wood on the riverbank. It places you on a fenced path that follows the edge of the wood and joins the old route at*.

Dinckley Footbridge. Photo: R.B.Evans

Until this big improvement to the route has been carried out, carry on as below, unless of course you want to visit Hurst Green for the sake of refreshments or visit Stonyhurst College. Turn to Section 4a if you wish to do so.

Go through the farmyard of Trough Farm and follow their access road to Hurst Green. Turn right to the Shireburn Arms and right again between the petrol pumps and the bus shelter. At the end of the buildings cross the stile onto a farm road, cross it and continue down the hedge side. Where the fence turns right, cross the little stream by the bridge and continue to follow the stream down the hill. As you approach the wood bear right to find the stile. On the other side of this narrow strip of boggy woodland you will find a well trodden path that takes you across a field then through more woodland* very steeply down to a footbridge across Lambing Clough and the banks of the Ribble. Turn left and follow the banks of the Ribble quite closely all the way to its junction with the Hodder near Winckley Hall Farm.

Brockhall, a hospital for the mentally disabled lies across the river, and close to the spot where the Calder joins the Ribble, Hacking Hall stands in a commanding position.

Follow the cart track by the Hodder into the complex of farm

Pendle Hill is a landmark along the Ribble Way. Here it is seen in the distance from Mitton Bridge. Photo: R.B.Evans

buildings. Follow their access road for perhaps ¼ mile - a delightful stretch in springtime with horse-chestnuts in bloom. As you approach some brick buildings on the right of the track, look for a hidden swing gate on the right. Now cut across the field to another one near a couple of big trees, then work diagonally right towards the wood.

As you top the rise of the field you will get a view of the cupolas of Stonyhurst College above the trees. They look as if they belong to some foreign land not the Ribble Valley. Wish you had taken the diversion for a better look? All is not lost.

Now follow the wood bearing left at its end to find the stile. The green gate ahead brings you onto the road a good mile from Great Mitton and opposite a lane that will take you to Stonyhurst in about 20 minutes, though it lacks the fine approach given by the route used in Section 4a. Turn right on the road. It has a footpath at first and then a wide grass verge, so is not bad going, but when you reach the first road on the right which is the direct road to Great Mitton, all this changes. This road is narrow and twisting and there are no grass verges. It carries quite a lot of traffic and is potentially dangerous for walkers. Take the greatest care, or if you are not in a hurry, continue for a ¼ mile to the other road (bus stop) to Great Mitton and use that. It is a little longer but much safer.

GREAT MITTON TO BRUNGERLEY BRIDGE

At Great Mitton[5] go past the café and garage and over the bridge to the Aspinall Arms. Here cross the stile just beyond the pub and shortly bear right up the field following the hedge. After crossing a small stream aim for the concrete bridge ahead. The electric fences barring the way have "gates" with insulated handles so there's no problem. Here you will find a stony cart track leading to a farm, whose access road you then follow along the riverside and past Clitheroe's waste disposal centre. Follow the road for about 1/4 mile until you have crossed a bridge, then at once turn left on a rough farm access road. It forks in about 100 yards where you will find the stile. Now follow the hedge to the left round two sides of the field, then drop down to the riverbank, here badly eroded by flood water. Two fields later you will enter Edisford Bridge[6] Caravan and Campsite.

As you leave it follow the tarmac path up to the road and continue along it for about 1/4 mile to the car park. Then take the access road to the Ribblesdale Pool. At the end of the buildings bear right across the playing fields aiming at the whitewashed buildings to find the way onto the road. Turn left then make a quick right turn into Union Street and carry on past the restored Wesleyan school into a rough lane. Continue beyond the allotment and in about 200 yards you will find a stile on your left.

Now make for the river ahead and you will arrive at or near the weir of the former Low Mill cotton factory.[7] From here there is a delightful riverside path to Brungerley Bridge.[6]

Things seen on the Way

This section of the walk is particularly rich in buildings of historical and architectural interest.

1. Stydd Church. This chapel is extremely small and simple and has an air of great antiquity. It belonged to a preceptory of the Knights Hospitallers and was built in the twelfth century. The knights were an order of crusading monks who were dissolved by Henry VIII and their preceptory has long since disappeared.

2. Stydd Almshouses. This curious Italianate building was erected by one of the Shireburn family in 1728 to house five poor people.

In summer the riverside park at Edisford Bridge is a popular attraction

The miniature railway at Edisford Bridge .
The steam engine rides draw children of all ages Photos: R.B.Evans

There are two dwellings on the ground floor and a wide stone staircase passes between them to reach a loggia with three more dwellings which are sheltered by a three-bay arcade of rustic Tuscan columns. They are still in use.

3.   Dinckley Hall and ferry. The white farm building is soon spotted as you approach the footbridge, but its most interesting architectural feature, its cruick-built south wall is best seen from the wood above - if there are not too many leaves on the trees. It is known to have been in existence since 1333. Like all the old halls along the Ribble it had its own ferry, which was replaced by the footbridge in October 1951 by Lancashire County Council.

4.   Hacking Hall. This venerable house is the largest and most elaborate of those close to the Ribble Way. It appears in the Coucher Book of Whalley Abbey of 1374 but the present house was rebuilt in 1607 by Thos Walmsley, then in his seventieth year. He lived at Dunkenhalgh near Clayton-le-Woods at the time and built it for his wife so that she could have her own residence after his death. It has been called a house of many gables - there are five under the front roof line. The projecting wings, mullioned windows and massive chimney breast on the south wall give it a most attractive appearance. Naturally it had its own ferry across the Ribble and the Calder and the ferryman lived in the house opposite. This ferry ran until 1954 and was of considerable value to walkers in the area. One of its old boats was discovered in a barn in 1983 and has been restored and is now housed in Clitheroe Castle Museum. This particular boat was about 12 feet long and could take 15 passengers, and was in use until 1938 when it was replaced.

5.   Great Mitton Church. Though slightly off route, the church has such a fine interior it is well worth visiting. It is usually locked during the week though the key may be obtained from the verger, who lives in the house at the church gate, if she is in. The church was built in the late thirteenth century and has had few structural alterations except the Shireburn Chapel, first built about 1440 and rebuilt in 1544 by Sir Richard Shireburn. He died the same year and this splendid chapel houses not only the alabaster effigies of Sir Richard and his wife Maud, but the no less splendid tombs of four more of the Shireburn family. It must be thought strange that the

family who lived at Stonyhurst should be buried at Great Mitton Church. It is simply that Stonyhurst, their manor house, was in the parish of Great Mitton, a huge one that extended from Hurst Green to Grindleton on the north side of the Ribble.

6. Clitheroe's bridges, Edisford, Brungerley, West Bradford and Grindleton are all either used by or are close to the Way. Edisford is by far the oldest, there has been a bridge there since 1339. West Bradford Bridge was built before 1822 but Grindleton was reached by ferry until 1855, and Brungerley Bridge was not built until 1816. Until that date the river was crossed by hipping (stepping) stones.

7. Low Moor housing estate. This modern estate, close to Edisford Bridge is on the site of the former Low Moor cotton factory. The factory was started in 1782 and was enlarged by the Garret and Horsefall families after the turn of that century. By 1841 it was a very large spinning and weaving mill with 238 houses and a Sunday school belonging to it. The mill and houses have all been demolished but the Sunday school still stands. The mill was built on the site to utilise the water power of the Ribble. The river was dammed below Waddow Hall[8] and a leat, still easily visible below the allotments, brought water to the factory. The mill had three water-wheels in 1830, later it installed a water turbine, and did not convert to steam until the 1890s. The great pool created by the dam was used as a boating lake in the 1870s.

8. Waddow Hall stands in a fine position above this pool and has belonged to the Girl Guides Association for many years.

Clitheroe
Clitheroe is a market town of considerable antiquity but apart from the castle keep and steward's house has no buildings of special interest. Nevertheless it has an appealing townscape and is well worth an hour or two. Ribble Valley Borough Council and Clitheroe Civic Society have jointly issued a pamphlet called *A Walk Through Clitheroe* that describes the best features in some detail. The most prominent feature of the town is, of course, the castle built on a limestone reef knoll about 1180 by Robert de Lacy who was Lord of the Honor of Clitheroe. The castle has had many changes of ownership over the centuries but finally both it and the grounds

were bought just after the World War I by the residents of the town, as a war memorial. The Castle Museum is housed in a fine late eighteenth-century house that was built for the Steward of the Honor of Clitheroe, just behind and below the keep of the castle, virtually all that remains today. The museum is well worth a visit and is open afternoons only, April to the end of October (small admission charge). As well as the displays of local history and industries ancient and modern that you would expect, there is a large gallery devoted to the geology of Ribblesdale. Besides the glittering specimens in the new mineral room, there is a large display with photographs and specimens entitled Roadside Geology, calculated to appeal to everybody, not just the geologically minded. A room devoted to the Salthill Quarry Geological Trail is a good deal more technical, and instructions are given for finding the quarry, no great distance from the town, but about 1¹/₂ miles along the road to regain the Way at West Bradford.

Clitheroe

Section 4a
OPTIONAL DIVERSION TO STONYHURST COLLEGE

Introduction

Allow about 2 hours for the whole diversion, more if you wish to have a look round some of the many rooms in the college which is open to the public during the months of July and August, 1.00-5.00pm (entry charge for a self-guided tour).

The route

Go straight up the access road from Trough Farm to Hurst Green, passing the Ribble Way stile that leaves this road on the right. Then go straight ahead up Avenue Road and past the Shireburn Almshouses, now known as Shireburn Cottages. You then enter a short stretch of unfenced road in woodland. Turn right at the end and the classic vista of Stonyhurst at the end of its long avenue of trees, lawns and lakes lies before you. The building seems distant, but keep going right until you come to the gateway where a notice states that the public are not allowed further. Enjoy the whole placid scene, the stately buildings in their fine setting, the mallard duck, the tame Canada geese, the rare black swan on one of the ornamental ponds.

When you have had your fill, turn right in front of the college. At the end of the buildings the road swings left. Leave it and go through the gate in the corner ahead. Aim for the far end of the wood where you will find the path. Follow the edge of the wood and then the hedge to find a swing gate and then a second one, but at the third turn left just BEFORE it. Now follow the hedge until it meets a wall, where you turn left and walk alongside to a short lane that will bring you into Avenue Road. Purists will retrace their steps to the point where the Way leaves the farm access road. Others may prefer to cut the corner by going down to the left of the Shireburn Arms between the petrol pumps and the bus shelter. At the end of the buildings cross the stile onto a farm access road and continue down by the hedge side. Where the fence turns right cross the little stream by the bridge and continue to follow the stream down the hill until you regain the Ribble Way.

62

Stonyhurst College. Photo: R.B.Evans

Stonyhurst College

The college is a well-known Roman Catholic public school and has been at Stonyhurst since 1794. The college was founded in France in Henry VIII's time in order to offer English Catholics the type of education denied them by him. During the French Revolution it was experiencing problems in France so the Weld family of Dorset (who inherited the Stonyhurst property) offered it to the school, who had just lost their own house. Stonyhurst has a very long history. The house was the manor house of the Shireburn family for at least 400 years until the line died out. Sir Richard Shireburn began to build a new house in 1592 and the present gatehouse is part of it. It can be seen quite well from the gateway marking the limit of public access. Generations of the family continued to live there, each making additions or alterations until the family died out in 1717 with the death of Sir Nicholas Shireburn. He was the man who built the two big cupolas, a landmark for miles around. He also laid out the grounds afresh making the avenue approach used in this book. Obviously the new owners of Stonyhurst started a repair and rebuilding programme to suit their needs, in particular the church between 1832 and 1835. In the mid-nineteenth century there was a boom in public school building and the next 40 years saw the main buildings as we see them today completed.

The self-guided tour takes you around classrooms, dormitories, the church, the old refectory which is part of the Elizabethan house built by Sir Richard Shireburn, the library with its 40,000 volumes, some of them very rare, and the museum, which houses some priceless relics of Renaissance times.

The Shireburns did not expend their entire wealth on their house at Stonyhurst. Like most wealthy families of the period they were concerned for the welfare of the poor and built the almshouses at Hurst Green in 1707. Originally they were on Kemple End, Longridge Fell and were moved from that unsuitable site and rebuilt in Hurst Green in 1946. The Shireburns, you may remember, built the almshouse near Ribchester. They built the village school in Hurst Green in 1686 but little of this building is left. Earlier members of the family built the Shireburn Chapel at Mitton Church, but some of the later clung to the old faith after the Reformation and suffered loss of lands and property as a result.

✳   ✳   ✳

*Stainforth Bridge, above, and Stainforth Force, below,
seen in summer low water. Photos: W.Unsworth*

The Way passes Thorns Gill, above, before reaching Gearstones, below. Photos: W.Unsworth

Section 5
BRUNGERLEY BRIDGE, CLITHEROE, TO GISBURN

Facts and facilities

Mileage: 10.5

Map: 1:50,000 Landranger Series Sheet No.103 Blackburn and Burnley

At Sawley

Toilets/Cafés/Shops: none

Pubs: one, passed on the Way

Telephone: on the road that leads to the A59

Bus Stop: on the A59

Parking: roadside by the river

At Gisburn

Toilets: close to the junction of the A59 and the Bolton by Bowland road

Pubs: three in the main street

Cafés: several

Shops: in the main street

P.O.:   opposite the Ribblesdale Arms

Telephone: on the Skipton side of the church

Bus Stop: in the main street by the post office

Parking: no car park. Room for a few cars near the toilets

The route

BRUNGERLEY BRIDGE TO SAWLEY

Turn right on the road and in about 100 yards you will come to the entrance to Brungerley Park. Stay on the lowest path in the park until you have passed a notice-board at the entrance to Cross Hill Quarry, a local nature reserve, then take the waymarked path on the

Clitheroe from the castle. Photo: R.Lowe

Sawley

left that follows the riverbank through the fields to West Bradford.

Here you are directly below the Ribblesdale Cement Works whose chimneys can be seen from many a mile away belching steam and smoke and whose rumblings and growlings bring back the industrial atmosphere of Preston to an otherwise charming bit of riverside. Noise is indeed a pollutant!

Cross the road and continue to follow the riverbank until the river starts to swing away to the left. Here you climb up a little and then follow a track between trees to the road between Chatburn and Grindleton. There are fine views of Pendle, standing grandly above the chimneys of Chatburn, and others up the river to Sawley. Turn left along the road and cross the bridge. At once turn right to the field at the signpost "Footpath to Rathmell Syke" and follow the flood bank of the river past the confluence of Swanside Beck. Then look for a stile in the hedge, turn right and when you meet the little brook turn left and follow it to the stile. Now go straight ahead up the hill for two-field-lengths to find the stile onto the road. Turn right and follow the road for about a mile to the Spread Eagle Hotel. Cut a corner to the bridge by going through a stile on the right opposite a row of cottages.

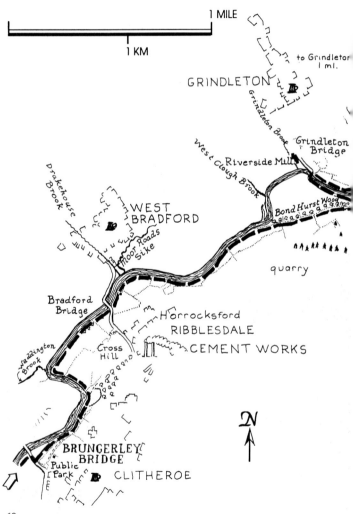

1 MILE

1 KM

to Grindleton
1 ml.

GRINDLETON

Grindleton Brook

Grindleton
Bridge

West Clough Brook

Riverside Mill

Bond Hurst Wood

Drakehouse Brook

WEST
BRADFORD

Moor Roads Sike

quarry

Bradford
Bridge

Horrocksford

RIBBLESDALE

CEMENT WORKS

Waddington Brook

Cross
Hill

𝒩

BRUNGERLEY
BRIDGE

Public
Park

CLITHEROE

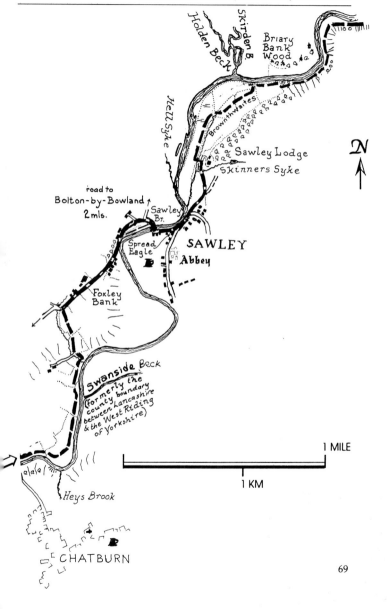

Holden Beck

Skirden B.

Briary Bank Wood

Hell Syke

Brownthwaites

Sawley Lodge

Skinners Syke

road to
Bolton-by-Bowland ↑
2 mls.

Sawley Br.

Spread Eagle

SAWLEY

Abbey

Foxley Bank

Swanside Beck

*formerly the
county boundary
between Lancashire
& the West Riding
of Yorkshire)*

Heys Brook

CHATBURN

𝒩

1 MILE

1 KM

69

SAWLEY TO GISBURN

Bear left at the pub and where the road swings right up the hill keep straight ahead through the ornamental stone gateway onto the private road to Sawley Lodge, ignoring the threatening notice. As you approach a similar gateway turn left through a sheepfold into a field. After about 100 yards turn left across a bridge over a ditch into the field. Turn right and follow a line of stiles until you meet the riverbank again at the entrance to Rainsber Wood.

TAKE CARE TO FOLLOW THIS SECTION CORRECTLY. It is very well waymarked so there is no excuse for wandering from the agreed route. Note, too, that you are forbidden to picnic and that this embargo extends to just beyond Rainsber Scar.

You are now starting the finest part of the Ribble Way. Sometimes the path goes close to the riverbank, sometimes it climbs quite steeply above it through the woods, sometimes through islands of pasture. Always it is utterly unspoilt, peaceful, serene, as the river flows in a deep cut valley

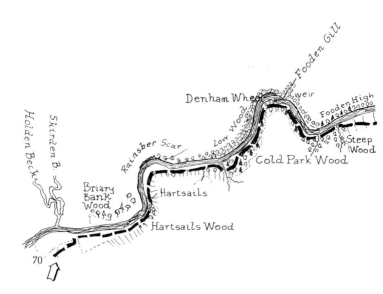

remote from the rest of the world. On a fine spring morning you may see the fish rising to fly, watch a water hen shepherd her brood of coal-black babies around the shallow margins, or be aroused from your daydreams by the quack-quack of a pair of mallards. Take care you do nothing to mar this marvellous bit of riverside.

Continue through this paradise until you have crossed a ladder stile, the first since entering the wood. Now bear right uphill, slightly away from the river. At first you follow a grassy bank which develops into a cart track. When the cart track ends you are on a grassy terrace above the river. Keep along it to find the stile on the right. Go up the field to cross the deep cut rivulet then return left and follow the fence to the top side of a barn where you will find a stile. Cross it, turn left and follow the hedge to the farm access road which you follow to a group of buildings. Turn left immediately before them to find a stile set back from the track. Now bear diagonally right to the field corner, then left to drop down to a tiny stream

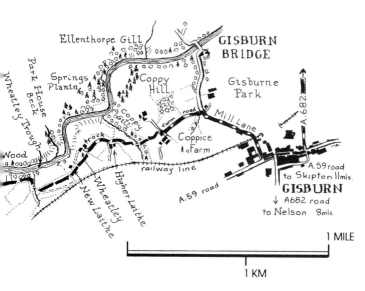

71

Sawley Abbey. Photo: R.Lowe

which you cross and go through a wicket gate into a belt of woodland. As you emerge from the wood keep straight ahead to find the stile to the left of the cottages. Turn right on the farm road and right again when you reach the public road. Ten minutes sees you into Gisburn, passing the toilets on the way.

Things seen on the Way

Cross Hill Quarry
Cross Hill Quarry, together with Salthill Quarry was worked extensively in the middle of the nineteenth century when there was a big demand for limestone to burn to quick lime for agricultural use and for use as a flux in the iron foundries of East Lancashire. Later in that century, even larger amounts were used as crushed stone for road building. The quarry was abandoned about 1900 and nature began to take over, if very slowly. Today both Cross Hill Quarry and Salthill Quarry are local nature reserves managed by the Lancashire Trust for Nature Conservation. There are several different soil types in the quarry and therefore a wide range of lime-loving flowers, including the rare bee orchid. Because of this, butterflies are plentiful, especially the common blue and the small tortoiseshell, though the much scarcer painted lady is also found in late summer.

Sawley Abbey

Sawley Abbey is quite often known as Salley Abbey, its original name. Like Whalley Abbey it was a Cistercian foundation and one could expect it to have been a daughter house of Whalley. This was not so. It was a daughter house of Fountains Abbey which owned a great deal of land in the Yorkshire Dales. It was founded in 1147, whereas Whalley was not established until 1216, rather late, because it had been at Stanlow, Cheshire in its early years. The gaunt ruins of the abbey are easily seen from the road corner by the Spread Eagle Hotel and though at first sight there is little left above ground there are surprisingly extensive foundations, laid bare by English Heritage. The Abbey was never wealthy like its parent house. Its lands were poor and the climate harsh and this is reflected in the quality of the stonework. There is very little ashlar masonry and large parts of the walls are simply built of crude stone blocks, some of it the very easily weathered Worston Shales, the cause of the gaunt and decrepit appearance of the remains. After the Dissolution of the Monasteries in 1536 much of the better stone was carted away and re-used, a common practice. Still worth a visit (entry fee).

Rainsber Scar

Rainsber Scar, the crag in the curve of the river, is the scene of Sir William Pudsay's leap. He was a coiner in the sixteenth century who made his own money from silver obtained from a mine on his own estate at Rimington. On discovery he fled from justice and it is said that to escape his pursuers he and his horse leapt the Ribble by jumping down the Scar. He was uninjured, made his escape and was eventually pardoned by Queen Elizabeth I.

Gisburn

Gisburn is a pleasant open village but lacks any buildings of note. Even the church, though superficially attractive hasn't got the interesting features of Mitton or Ribchester. The village's main claim to modest fame is that Gisburn Hall has been the home of the Lister family for almost 200 years. The Listers became Lords of Ribblesdale in 1797 and the first lord is said to have planted more than a million oak trees on his property, and a later one saw to it that the railway line, built in the 1880s, went through a tunnel where it passed close to the house and park.

The Ribble near Sawley. Photo: R.Lowe

Section 6
GISBURN TO SETTLE

Facts and facilities

Mileage: 10

Maps: 1:25,000 Outdoor Leisure Series Nos.2 and 10
1:50,000 Landranger Series Sheets No.103 Blackburn
and Burnley and No.98 Wensleydale and Wharfedale

At Paythorne

Pub: the Way passes it

Telephone: opposite the pub

Campsite: keep straight along the road to find it.
No other facilities, but obviously, no parking problem

At Halton West

Shop and P.O.: keep right on the road, ¹/₄ mile

At Rathmell

Telephone: opposite the church
No other facilities

At Settle

Toilets: in the car park close to the railway bridge on the A65
and under the Council Offices in the main street

Pubs/Cafés/Shops: plenty of these. Early closing day is
Wednesday

P.O.:   at the back of the Council Offices

Bus Stop: opposite the Council Offices

Parking: see toilets, also in the Market Place

Note:
This section of the walk is much less walked than the ones you have
already done. There are few well trodden paths but it is adequately

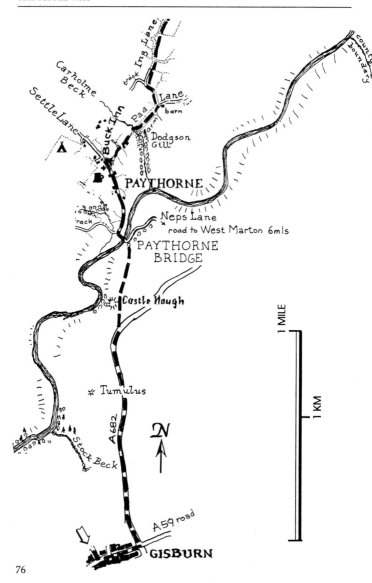

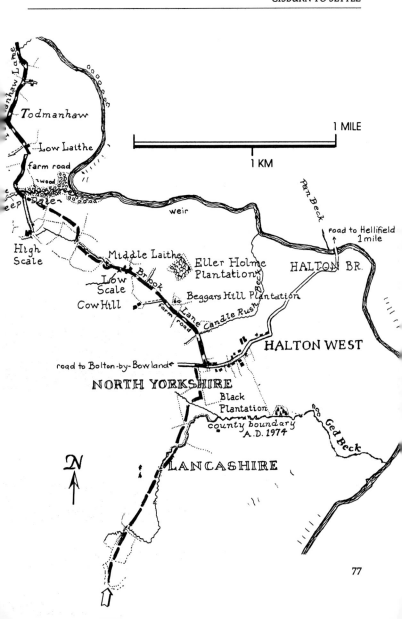

Todmanhaw

Low Laithe

farm road

wood

eep Dale

weir

1 MILE

1 KM

Pan Beck

road to Hellifield
1 mile

High
Scale

Middle Laithe

Eller Holme
Plantation

HALTON BR.

Low
Scale

Brook

Beggars Hill Plantation

Cow Hill

Lane

Candle Rush

farm road

HALTON WEST

road to Bolton-by-Bowland

NORTH YORKSHIRE

Black
Plantation

Ged Beck

county boundary
A.D. 1974

𝒩

LANCASHIRE

waymarked whilst you remain in Lancashire. In Yorkshire it's a different tale: you will rarely find a Ribble Way marker (though there are other waymarks) except where the path crosses a road. Route-finding can therefore be tricky.

The route

GISBURN TO HALTON WEST

Continue through Gisburn and turn left along the A682 immediately after the church. Follow this not unpleasant road - provided there isn't much traffic - for about 1¹/₂ miles. Then keep a lookout for Castle Haugh on your left. It's quite close, a large, flat-topped knoll surrounded by trees. Just before you reach it, the road makes a swing to the right, and you will see a gate, stile, finger post and waymark all together. Aim for a little gate just to the right of Castle Haugh where you find yourself on the edge of the great ditch that once surrounded this early Norman castle that safeguarded a crossing place on the Ribble. Now follow the fence into the wood where a wide path leads you down to the road at Paythorne Bridge. Turn left and continue up the hill to the Buck Inn, Paythorne.[1]

Almost opposite the pub is the bridleway to Nappa Flats, a good farm access road. Go along it for about 10 minutes and when you come to a cattle grid by a solitary barn, turn left into a grass lane between earth banks, much overgrown and not obvious at present. Follow this, using the diversion onto the edge of the field, until signs direct you to a right turn into a field where the lane, now green, continues, and follow its right bank. In due course it becomes gravelled and almost at once makes a sharp right turn. Here you keep straight ahead over the stile aiming for the right-hand end of a row of straggly hawthorn trees to find another stile. After crossing a further stile you start the moor proper, a large area of wet, rush-grown, rough grazing, across which a number of streams lazily meander. Now follow the direction indicated by the frequent waymarks to locate the bridges across these streams, which can be quite large in wet weather. After some apparent wandering about you will come to a bridge in a hedge; this is the Lancashire-Yorkshire border and the end of the moor. This bridge has a yellow arrow as waymark, not the familiar Ribble Way logo, and now you are in Yorkshire you will find these from time to time. Go through the gate ahead and make towards Halton West, which is now quite near. At the next hedge turn left to find the stile and a faint path will lead you onto the road.

HALTON WEST TO COW BRIDGE, LONG PRESTON

Turn right and 50 yards away you will see a finger post "Bridleway to Deep Dale". Turn up this lane and follow it to Low Scale Farm. As you approach the farm look for a sign diverting you to the left to go round the farmyard. Rejoin the main track just beyond the farm and continue along it until you are almost at the barn, then turn left into the field and pass behind it. Go through the gate ahead and follow the stream. At the next gate, which bears a N.Y.C.C. notice to the effect that the path has been diverted, simply follow the direction shown by the waymark at every stile, eventually aiming for the next gate to the wood to reach a farm access road. Turn right on this and right again when you reach the public road close to Cow Bridge.

Though tarmac, this is no bad thing for a while. The mind can relax and enjoy the scene. The hills behind Long Preston are just coming into view and one can detect with some satisfaction the long hollow in which the Ribble runs. It has been so long out of sight it might well be out of mind. In springtime the banks of the lane are a delight, thick with primroses. I beg of you not to pick them but leave them for others to enjoy.

COW BRIDGE TO RATHMELL

Follow the well-marked path from the finger post "To Rathmell" along the banks of the Ribble, at last regained, then to the left along Wigglesworth Beck. You will join a gravel farm track just before Wigglesworth Hall Farm. Go straight ahead on it, bear right through the gate, cross the bridge and then turn left onto the farm's access road. As soon as you have crossed the cattle grid turn right, cross the little stream and climb up to a stile. Now pass by the electricity supply pole and drop down to rejoin the main farm cart track. Follow this until it starts to climb away to the left towards a couple of trees. Here you go almost straight ahead to a stile that is out of sight. Go straight across the field below the wall to a corner, turn left and follow the fence to the wood. At the wood turn right and you

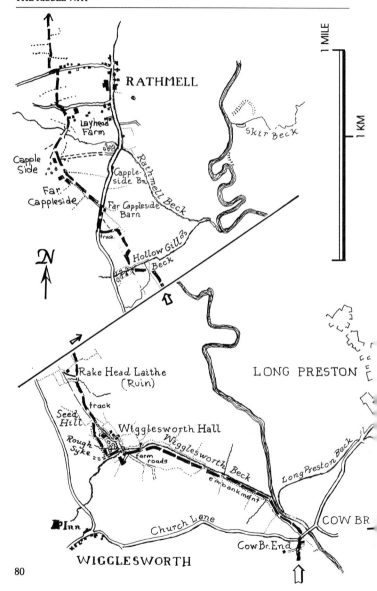

RATHMELL

Layhead Farm

Capple Side

Far Cappleside

Cappleside Bn

Rathmell Beck

Skir Beck

Far Cappleside Barn

track

Hollow Gill Beck

N

Rake Head Laithe (Ruin)

track

Seed Hill

Wigglesworth Hall

Rough Syke

Wigglesworth Beck

farm roads

LONG PRESTON

Long Preston Beck

embankment

Inn

Church Lane

COW BR

Cow Br. End

WIGGLESWORTH

1 MILE

1 KM

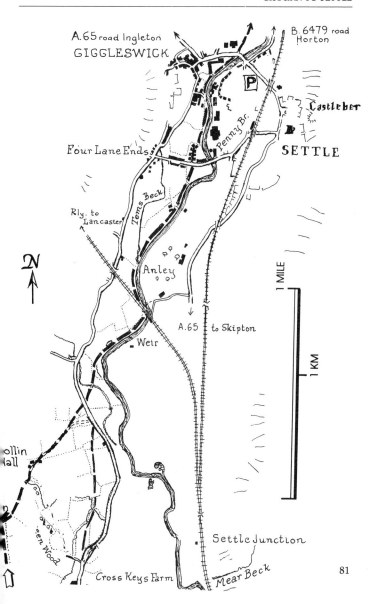

A.65 road Ingleton
GIGGLESWICK

B.6479 road
Horton

P

Castleber

SETTLE

Four Lane Ends

Penny Br.

Tems Beck

Rly. to
Lancaster

Anley

N

1 MILE

1 KM

Weir

A.65 to Skipton

ollin
all

en Wood

Settle Junction

Cross Keys Farm

Mear Beck

81

Monastic remains at Wigglesworth Hall

will find a new bridge over the stream. On the other side turn right at the new post and wire fence and follow it to a gate on to the road, a short mile from Rathmell.

RATHMELL TO SETTLE

Turn right on the road and after about 200 yards turn left into the farm access road leading to Far Cappleside. Just before the corner turn right over a stile, cut across to a stile by the wood then make for the road leading to Cappleside, a fine early Victorian house.[2] You'll find a red plastic handle in the electric fence so that you can go through it. Now keep straight ahead past the farm buildings, then pick up a hollow way that leads you down to the little pack horse bridge over Rathmell Beck, a delightful spot. Turn right in the lane beyond, and at the top of the rise go slightly left into a green lane. After 30 yards or so leave it for a slit stile on the right. Now follow the wall on the right to its corner then keep straight ahead to a slit stile, and straight ahead again to find a little gate by a sycamore tree to reach the road opposite Rathmell School. Turn left on the road and in a few yards or so you will see the Ribble Way logo at a slit stile into a well kept field: the school playing field. Keep straight on towards a large barn where you will find the stile on its left. Now follow the wall on the right to a stile in a corner which puts you onto a lane. Turn right through the little hamlet then keep straight ahead passing through two gates in quick succession to reach the field. Go down the field towards the farm where you will find a slit stile in the wall. Go forwards through the buildings then turn right on the farm access road which you follow almost to the road. When you are nearly there keep a look out for a stone step stile on the left. Use this to cut the corner and reach the road opposite the signpost and stile to Settle. From it a faint path leads diagonally left to find a flat bridge to the right of a solitary hawthorn tree. You need that bridge. Then make for a short length of wall in a hedgerow to find the next stile. From it you can see the Ribble again. Make for it, go under the railway bridge and follow it almost into Settle.

This is a delightful stretch of river - close-cropped turf, a fine line of mature beech trees probably planted 130 years ago by the owners of Anley House, the fine house visible from the road. All, of course, provided you keep your eyes turned right. The leftward and forward views are not attractive.

As you are approaching the road the river swings right, but you keep straight ahead to a little swing gate onto the road. If you want to visit Settle turn right on the road and follow it to the town centre in about 10 minutes. Otherwise go straight across the road to find a

Cattle drinking from the river, are a familiar sight. Photo: R.B.Evans

narrow tarmac path between two bungalows. This will lead you into a close of new houses where you continue ahead, passing to the left of No.36 to find a path that leads you to the riverbank, which you reach via the rugby field. Stay on the riverbank path right to Settle Bridge on the A65. If you have been into Settle[3] already, pick up the Way at this point.

Things seen along the Way

1.   Paythorne is one of the very few villages in North Lancashire that is mentioned in Domesday Book (AD 1086). Castle Haugh, close to the main road, A682, is almost certainly the site of an early Norman motte and bailey castle, built of wood, not stone. Perhaps Paythorne's greatest claim to local fame is Salmon Sunday, the third in November, when crowds of people from East Lancashire used to gather to watch the annual 'running' of the salmon to the spawning beds high up the river. Pollution mainly from the Calder and Darwen became so great in the postwar years that the salmon no longer came in quantity, but now pollution has been reduced sufficiently to allow them to run again in number. If the time of year is right and you want to have a look, turn right on the road by the

pub and follow it to the river bridge.

2. Cappleside, a well proportioned house in the late Georgian style, was built in 1832 by the Geldard family. As you pass, you may note the wide unobstructed vista it enjoys across the Ribble Valley, enhanced by the ha-ha, not a wall, that ends the lawn. Behind it is another house built around and masking a much earlier house, probably of the mid-seventeenth century.The barn has a datestone of 1732, just visible from the track, and the elaborate building to its right was built in 1898 as a stable block with a meeting room in the top storey.

3. Settle is another place of ancient origin with a satisfying "higgledy-piggledy" market place. But the oldest part of the town lies in the steep lanes of Upper Settle. The Craven Museum is on one of these, Victoria Street, and has some items from the building of the Settle-Carlisle railway. The Way goes along the riverbank giving a good view of a one-time water-powered cotton mill, now used for farm storage. It took its water from the weir whose remains can be seen just below the bridge on the A65. At the other end of this bridge there is another former cotton mill whose weir and water-wheel are still there. Langcliffe Mill, well seen on the next section of the Way is another of these early mills. They seem a long way indeed from Preston and its cotton mills, and the reason for their establishment was two-fold: the availability of abundant water power and the arrival of the Leeds and Liverpool canal at Gargrave in the early years of the nineteenth century which enabled cotton to reach the water power much more cheaply.

Section 7
SETTLE TO HORTON-IN-RIBBLESDALE

Facts and facilities
Mileage: 8

Maps: 1:25,000 Outdoor Leisure Series Nos.2 and 10

At Stainforth
Toilets: in the car park on the bypass

Pub: one in the village

Café/Shop: in the village opposite the pub

P.O.: on the road leading to Goat Scar Lane

Telephone: at the back of the village, signposted by the shop

Bus Stop: by the pub

Parking: see toilets

At Horton-in-Ribblesdale
Toilets: in the car park near the river bridge

Pubs: two

Café: the well known Peny-y-ghent Café, a mecca for all walkers, on the main road just south of the car park

Shop: with the post office

P.O.: close to the Pennine Way path to Pen-y-ghent

Telephone: between the café and the car park

Bus Stop: opposite the café

Parking: see toilets

The route
The signposted path to Stackhouse starts across the road. Follow it round the edge of the Settle School's playing fields[1] to a stone step

A turbulent fall on the river at Settle

stile then through fields above the river to the road. It is well used and has fine views across the river to Pen-y-ghent. Turn right on the road and follow it for a few hundred yards until you come to a white house on the right. Turn right here and follow a narrow lane to the river. The weir and salmon ladder are worth a moment, then turn left and follow the riverbank all the way to the old pack horse bridge[2] at Little Stainforth. This is a very fine stretch of river scenery with a splendid little climax of deep pools and a waterfall just below the pack horse bridge. The path is well marked most of the way. When you are approaching the caravan site go over the ladder stile to the riverbank and follow it to the bridge. You'll pass waterfalls and a fine, deep pool, just right for a dip on a hot day - if you are a good swimmer. Turn right over the bridge, right again when you reach the main road, then first left to reach Stainforth. Continue past the car park, turn left at the road junction, and go along a narrow lane between the houses at the point where the road turns right. You will see a finger post to Moor Head Lane. Once in the second field strike diagonally right steeply up the hill to the wall corner. Then follow the little beck for a while until you can see a ladder stile ahead. Now keep in this general straight line through large fields of

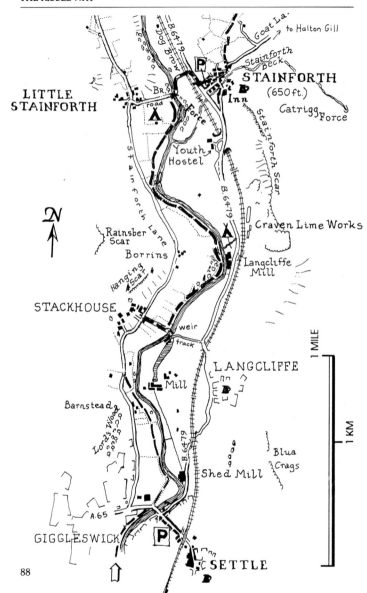

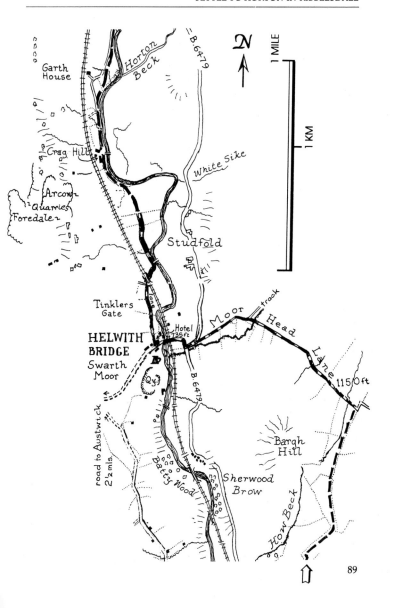

N

1 MILE

1 KM

Garth
House

Horton Beck

B.6479

Crag Hill

White Sike

Arcow
Quarries
Foredale

Studfold

Tinklers
Gate

Moor Head Lane

Hotel
735 ft

HELWITH
BRIDGE

Swarth
Moor

B.6479

1150 ft

road to Austwick
2½ mls.

Batty Wood

Sherwood
Brow

Bargh
Hill

How Beck

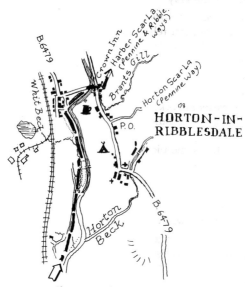

rough pasture until you reach Moor Head Lane. Turn left and go steeply downhill, facing the great scar of the quarries above Helwith Bridge, an appalling blot on the landscape of a national park, but a fine opportunity to study the geology of this part of Ribblesdale.[3] Turn left on the rough lane below and continue to the Settle-Horton road. Carry on a couple of hundred yards down this road to the turning to Helwith Bridge. Go past the pub where you cut across the corner of a field to reach a rough road leading to the quarries. Follow this to the railway bridge, pass under it and continue into a narrow walled lane which becomes very wet, sometimes waterlogged in places. It ends rather vaguely in a large field where you go straight ahead past a straggly line of trees to reach the banks of the Ribble once more. Now turn left and simply follow the river to the road bridge at Horton, passing to the right of Cragghill Farm just ahead. There's a pleasant well marked path with good views of Pen-y-ghent all the way. If you want to visit Horton, the *wooden* bridge where the riverside path ends brings you direct to the car park. If not, then cross the *road* bridge and turn left by the Crown.

Things seen on the Way

1. The mill by the river so well seen from the footpath just past the playing fields is another relic of the Industrial Revolution around Settle. It is one of the oldest and took its water supply from the weir and mill pond at Langcliffe.

2. The ancient pack horse bridge over the Ribble at Stainforth now belongs to the National Trust. It was on the old pack horse route that ran from Lancaster to York in Tudor times. No doubt it replaced an earlier river crossing as indicated by the "forth" part of the village's name.

Stainforth has some picturesque corners including stepping-stones across Stainforth Beck, whereas Horton has lost all its charm in Victorian villas, railway cottages and modern bungalows. The church makes up for it: a fine building retaining some of its early Norman work, for it was sensitively restored in Victorian times, whereas Stainforth's was virtually rebuilt.

3. If you are interested in geology take a closer look at the quarrying at Helwith Bridge. Exactly what you see depends on the current state of quarrying. Two things are clear: the quarried rock is not limestone like the little crag perched above it and the rock strata sweeps up nearly vertically whereas the limestone's is horizontal. The material of the vertical strata is an ancient Silurian Slate, a Pre-Cambrian rock found from Settle almost to Horton at the bottom of the valley. Above Horton the valley floor is limestone which is quarried at Horton.

Section 8
HORTON-IN-RIBBLESDALE TO THE SOURCE

Facts and facilities

Mileage: 6.5 to Ribblehead, 10.5 to the source

Map: 1:25,000 Outdoor Leisure Series No.2

Facilities are almost non-existent. The Station Hotel at
Ribblehead is a good mile away

The route

HORTON TO RIBBLEHEAD

If you have come from Horton itself, cross the first road bridge then
turn up a walled lane[1] to the right of the Crown, it's signed as the
Pennine Way as well as the Ribble Way. Follow the lane as far as Sell

Pen-y-ghent from above Horton

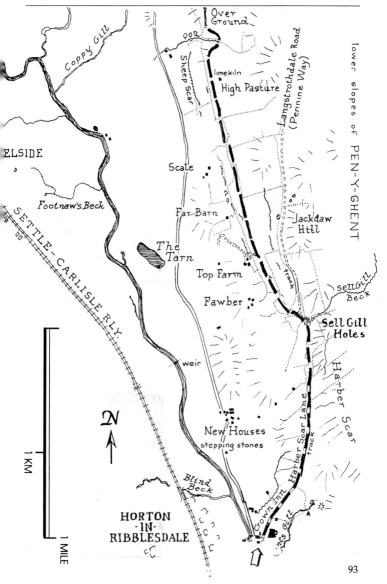

Over Ground

Coppy Gill

Sheep Scar

limekiln

High Pasture

Langstrothdale Road (Pennine Way)

lower slopes of PEN-Y-GHENT

ELSIDE

Scale

Footnaw's Beck

SETTLE - CARLISLE RLY.

Far Barn

The Tarn

Top Farm

Fawber

Jackdaw Hill

track

Sell Gill Beck

Sell Gill Holes

weir

Harber Scar

N

1 KM

1 MILE

New Houses

stepping stones

Harber Scar Lane

track

Crown Inn

Sell Gill

Blind Beck

HORTON-IN-RIBBLESDALE

93

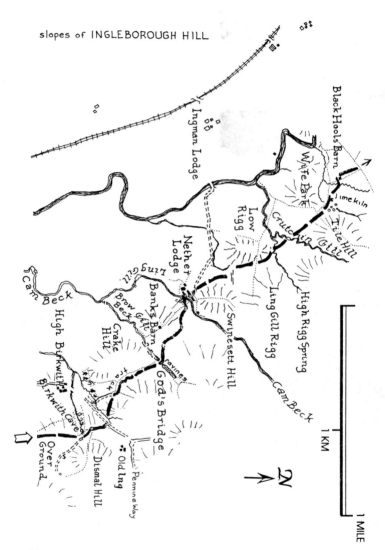

slopes of INGLEBOROUGH HILL

Ingman Lodge

Black Hools Barn

White Park

Lime kiln

Low Rigg

Crutchin Gill

Tite Hill

Nether Lodge

Ling Gill

Ling Gill Rigg

High Rigg Spring

Cam Beck

Banks Barn

Brow Beck

Crake Hill

High Birkwith

Swinesett Hill

Cam Beck

Birkwith Cave

God's Bridge

ravines

Over Ground

Old Ing

Dismal Hill

Pennine Way

N

1 KM

1 MILE

94

God's Bridge

Gill Barn, the first building on the left reached after crossing a sizeable stream,[2] which may be dry in summer. Turn left here crossing a ladder stile and turn right immediately below the barn. The stiles are obvious through three short fields and then you enter a very long one. At its end there is a stile high on the right, but you keep below the wall corner following the wall to find the next ladder stile, which is crucial for locating the crossing place of a deep cut gill just before you reach the gill of Birkwith Cave.[3] It's a couple of field lengths from this stile. The walls of the gill seem precipitous but a little path takes you down to the footbridge. Then make towards the wall above the plantation around Birkwith Cave and continue to a gate, just beyond which you reach the High Birkwith - Old Ing farm road.

Opposite, a faint path crosses the hillside to join the main track where it emerges from a gate. Shortly you will cross God's Bridge[4] then simply follow this well marked track to Nether Lodge,[5] going between the house and farm buildings onto their access road. Here you will find a multi-armed signpost. Go straight ahead to

95

*The Way crosses Thorns Gill, a pretty little limestone ravine,
near Gearstones*

Approaching Birkwith along the limestone shelf. Typical Dales barns are seen. Whernside, shrouded in mist, lies at the head of the valley

Ribblehead, a few yellow-topped posts starting you off in the right direction. A well trodden little path soon develops and takes you to the first stile where you bear left to cross Crutchin Gill, sometimes dry in summer. Continue to a barn, turn right and go over the hill and down to Black Hools barn. Over the second ladder stile turn left and then right through a gateway with a blob of yellow paint. There was no path to follow in 1991, so follow the wall at first, pass an isolated ash tree on its left and keep straight ahead to a wall corner. Now you may find a faint path going diagonally left down to the fragile little pack horse bridge over Thorns Gill, the finest gill of them all, its brown peaty waters tumbling from pool to pool in the water-worn limestone rocks. Continue up the field to reach the Ingleton-Hawes road.

RIBBLEHEAD TO THE SOURCE

Turn right and follow the road for about 400 yards to the Dales Way signpost on the track to Winshaw, for the Ribble Way now uses the route of the Dales Way as far as the Newby Head - Dent road. Pass to the left of the houses, turn right at the wall corner above, and

The source of the Ribble

follow this wall that divides the moor from the fields below. At its end continue along a well marked but very boggy track that contours the moor at the foot of the steeper ground. At the Newby Head - Dent road turn right and continue to the Ingleton-Hawes road junction. The Ribble Way starts the last lap from a signpost about 100 yards to the left of the junction. There's no path across the rough moor to start with, simply bear right climbing a little and keeping parallel to the road and you will soon pick it up. (It is, in fact, visible from the road junction and is much more easily reached from there.) The path soon becomes a rough cart track and swings left around the shoulder of the moor into Long Gill, to a little concrete building used to store animal fodder. The path continues, quite well marked, up the gill to its junction with Jam Sike. Here it crosses and follows the left bank of that gill which curves round to the right and eventually goes underground - for you have now reached the limestone strata - except in winter or wet weather. A number of small springs appear here and there, but keep going up to the wall. Turn right and follow it past a gateway blocked with piled-up concrete blocks. Just a little further is the highest spring of all, burbling forth in a most satisfying manner from the foot of a little rocky bank, and running even in summer. This spring, at an altitude of just over 1,800 feet is surely the true source of the Ribble.

RETURN TO CIVILISATION

The easiest way back to Horton-in-Ribblesdale is by the Pennine Way. (It is of course equally easy to get to Hawes if that suits your plans.) The problem at the moment is getting to the Pennine Way. There is no right of way path linking the end of the Ribble Way to the Pennine Way and all possible ways involve crossing unstable limestone walls, very nasty indeed. The author cannot recommend these and you are left with no alternative but to retrace your steps to the road, go down it for a couple of miles, and take the Dales Way up the moor again to reach the Pennine Way on Cam End. Yorkshire Dales Outdoor Leisure Map No.2 makes this clear.

Things seen on the Way

1. Sell Gill Lane was the original road up the valley and joined the Lancaster-Richmond road on Dodd Fell.

2. In normal weather Sell Gill disappears in the stream bed above the cart track in a quite dramatic manner, forming Sell Gill Pot. This pothole was explored as early as 1897 by the Yorkshire Ramblers' Club who found a deep shaft leading into a huge cavern, considered to be Yorkshire's second largest - the largest being the Main Chamber of Gaping Gill. Below the road there is another entrance, a cave-cum-shaft which leads to the same cavern. The pothole has a total depth of 210 feet.

3. Birkwith Cave is at the head of the ravine and a sizeable stream issues from it. There is a stile into the ravine on the farm side of it and it is not difficult to get down to the cave, the mouth of which is impressively large, but it quickly becomes impossible. Directly across the valley a small plantation of conifers above Selside marks

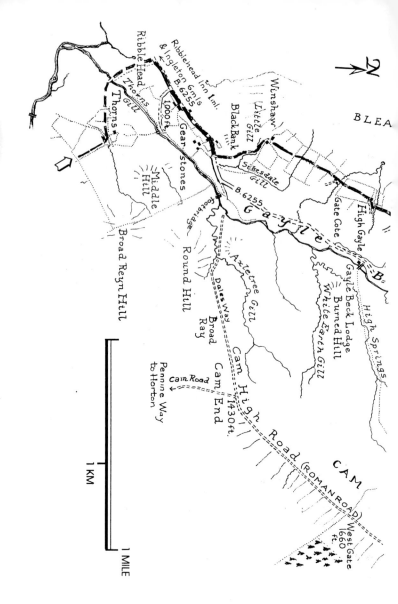

Ribble Head

Thorns

Thorns Gill

Ribblehead Inn 6m/s
& Ingleton B.6255

Ribblehead Inn 6m/s
& Ingleton B.6255

Winshaw

Little
Gill

Black Bank

BLEA

100 ft.

Gear
Stones

Sikesdale
Gill

B.6255

Ga   yle

footbridge

Gate Gate

High Gayle

"B"

Middle
Hill

Broad Reyn Hill

Round Hill

Axletree Gill

Dales Way

Broad
Ray

Gayle Beck Lodge
Burned Hill
White Earth Gill

High Springs

Cam High Road

Cam Road

Pennine Way
to Horton

Cam End
1430 ft.

Cam Road (Roman Road)

CAM

West Gate
1660 ft.

1 KM

1 MILE

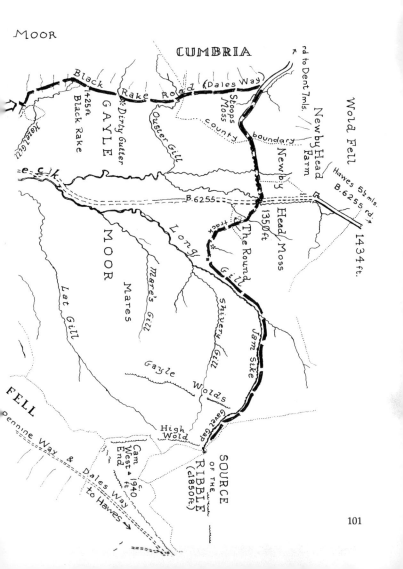

MOOR

CUMBRIA

Black Rake Road (Dales Way)

Stoops Moss

rd to Dent 7mls. ↗

Newby Head Farm

Wold Fell

GAYLE

Black Rake

+425ft

Dirty Gutter

Ouster Gill

county boundary

Newby

Hazel Gill

e c k

B.6255

Long

Newby Head Moss

1350ft

Hawes 5½ mls.
B.6255 rd ↑

1434 ft.

MOOR

Mare's Gill

Mares

The Round

track

Gill

Lat Gill

Gayle

Wolds

Shivery Gill

Jam Sike

FELL

Pennine Way & Dales Way to Hawes ➤

High Wold

Cam West ▲1940 ft. End

Gavel Gap

SOURCE OF THE RIBBLE (c1850 ft.)

Sell Gill pothole

the position of Alum Pot.

4. God's Bridge is a natural limestone bridge over the deep cut stream, so massive it is hardly recognisable as a bridge.

5. The numerous little hillocks crossed by the Way just after Nether Lodge are drumlins, heaps of debris left by the retreating glaciers of the last Ice Age.

* * *

103